Invitation to
TEACHING

INVITATION SERIES

Invitation to
TEACHING

Trevor Kerry

BASIL BLACKWELL

9573

© Trevor Kerry 1986

First published 1986

Basil Blackwell Ltd
108 Cowley Road, Oxford OX4 1JF, UK

Basil Blackwell Inc.
432 Park Avenue South, Suite 1503
New York, NY 10016, USA

British Library Cataloguing in Publication Data
Kerry, Trevor
    Invitation to Teaching.——(Invitation
    series)
    1. Teaching——Vocational guidance——Great
    Britain
    I. Title
    371.1'02'02341   LB1775
    ISBN 0-631-15019-6
    ISBN 0-631-15021-8 Pbk

Library of Congress Cataloging in Publication Data
Kerry, Trevor.
    Invitation to teaching.
    (Invitation series)
    Bibliography: p.
    Includes index.
    1. Teaching. 2. Teaching——Vocational guidance.
    3. Education——Great Britain. I. Title. II. Series.
    LB1025.2.K45 1986   371.1   86-9610
    ISBN 0-631-15019-6
    ISBN 0-631-15021-8 (pbk.)

Typeset by Columns of Reading
Printed in Great Britain by Whitstable Litho, Kent

Contents

Acknowledgements

The author acknowledges the permission granted by the following publishers to reproduce material previously published: Holt-Saunders Ltd (figure 3.1, p. 33; figure 3.2, p. 40; figure 3.3, p. 47; figure 3.4, p. 51; from *Psychology and the Teacher* by D. Child); Routledge and Kegan Paul (pp. 83–4; from *Social Class, Language and Education* by Dennis Lawton); Macmillan, London and Basingstoke ('Profile of a Teacher', p. 140; from *Mixed Ability Teaching* by Trevor Kerry and M. K. Sands); *Times Educational Supplement*, 7 February 1986 (table 12.2, pp. 202–5).

Introduction

This book is intended for those who are interested in exploring teaching as a career. Many of its readers will be young people trying to decide how best to plan a route into the profession. A few may be rather older, and they are likely to be seeking a new outlet for existing qualifications and skills. I have tried to bear both of the audiences in mind when writing the book, and to present as broad a view of the profession as possible.

Teaching can offer quite a varied career to anyone who wishes to take advantage of opportunities to undertake in-service training, to widen his or her own repertoire, and to move from one geographical location to another or from one branch or age range of teaching to another.

The book sets out to examine the nature of teaching and its practice – that is, what teachers do – but it begins by taking an inevitably cursory glance at the kinds of professional knowledge teachers have to have.

Chapter 1 begins at the centre of teaching activity by visiting a classroom. It is a real classroom, though all the names have been changed. This teacher and her class were originally studied by me as part of an extensive piece of research carried out for the 'Developing Pupils' Thinking Through Topic Work' project under the auspices of the Schools' Council. This opening chapter looks at a primary classroom since this is the early experience of education for all children. However, later chapters take up the themes in secondary and higher education settings. I have used this primary material in a narrative form here to help set the scene for the book.

Chapters 2–6 deal with the kinds of professional knowledge that teachers need, regardless of subject specialism, to do their jobs. Chapter 2 is a rapid glance at the history of education in Britain until about 1970. More recent events are dealt with incidentally in other chapters. Chapters 3 and 4 look at the distinctive contribution made by psychology to education and teaching. The first of these chapters is an outline of some essential psychological knowledge for teachers. The second looks at how psychologists and psychology can illuminate both the material taught in school and also help in the better care of the child.

In chapter 5 the perspective shifts to sociology. Because there is such a vast literature on the sociology of education, most of it less than thirty years old, no attempt is made to summarize what might be the basic components of a sociology of education course. Instead, a number of studies are examined in some detail to illuminate the methods of sociology and the relevance of its findings to education and teaching. Finally, among the more theoretical chapters, chapter 6 takes a reflective and more philosophical glance at some issues and values in contemporary education.

Chapters 7–9 put the reader in the role of teacher and give the flavour of the job. The infant and junior school sectors are described in chapter 7. The next chapter illustrates the role of the teacher in today's comprehensive schools. Chapter 9 looks at possibilities for teaching older students and adults in college or university settings.

Training for teaching is discussed in chapter 10, where the reader will find a detailed outline of a typical BEd course and some thoughts on the degree-plus-PGCE route into the profession. Chapter 11 asks you to try to assess how suitable you feel you will be in tackling the typical roles a teacher may be called upon to play both inside and outside the classroom. Finally, chapter 12 is devoted to the practical issues of how to apply for a place at a training college; and it also takes a look at the longer-term career options open to teachers.

A section called Notes on the Chapters has been added so that those who wish to do so may follow up some of the references made in the text. The text itself has been kept clear of formal references to make it easier and quicker to read.

This is a biased book. It is written by someone who has been a teacher for over twenty years and who has spent varying periods of time in primary and secondary schools, on the staff of colleges of education and a university, in further education, and as an educational researcher. It begins from the proposition that teaching is a worthwhile and rewarding way to spend one's life, and preaches throughout the twin gospels of professionalism and enthusiasm as the only valid approaches to the task.

1

Let's Visit a Classroom

Hipstone is a large red-brick primary school in a red-brick Georgian and Victorian town. As the town has expanded in recent times so has the school. Modern flat-roofed classrooms are linked to the original buildings by open-sided, wind-swept walkways. The austerity is relieved in part by the green expanse of the playing field and by the shrubby patios of the newer areas of the school. In part, the Victorian tiled corridors are mellowed by colourful displays of pupils' work: paintings, friezes, collages, poems and *objets trouvées*.

The pupils in Mrs Roberts' class are re-assembling after morning break. They are bubbly 8–9 year-olds, returning to their busy classroom with as much enthusiasm as they showed on leaving it to play football or tag, or to spend their pennies at the tuck-shop over the breaktime. Without prompting, the youngsters return quickly to their working groups and settle to their respective tasks.

All the work the pupils are engaged in relates to a recent visit to the local village of Cornham. Here, the youngsters mapped the village layout, walked all its streets and paths, studied the ages and designs of the houses, visited a farm, and handled the log book of the ancient village school. They studied the census returns for 1850 noting how many people lived in the village, what jobs they did, how many children they had, and how long they lived. Now the teacher has provided some follow-up studies to reinforce this learning, and also to encourage the youngsters to empathize with the people of that time and to use their knowledge to make

4

deductions and conclusions. It seems a tall order for 8-year-olds; but the following paragraphs show how it does really work in practice.

The children are divided into five main groups. Group 1 has been supplied by the teacher wth the yoke and leather fittings from the horse-trappings of an ancient plough or farm cart. The group knows in principle what the objects are; but they have been set two tasks – to describe them in detail using a classification system for man-made objects and to work out how they fitted onto the horse. Using the classification system is common practice in this school, so the pupils fall easily to the task. They run over the questions, answering each in turn:

Is the object living or non-living;
               organic or inorganic;
               animal, plant, mineral?
Is it to supply animal or human needs?
What is it made from?
What needs does it meet?

Eventually they begin to tackle the question: How was the object used? This is where their deductive or reasoning skills come in, and for the moment we will leave them to wrestle with the problem.

Just as the teacher has provided group 1 with materials and a problem, so she has set group 2 to work. Cornham village boasted a windmill, and this has led to speculation about the wind as a source of power. Pupils in group 2 have each been given some sticks, some brass tacks and some stout paper. The idea is to use the paper to design and build sails for a windmill in a variety of forms. The sails are to be attached to the sticks, the sticks set up on the playing field, and the efficiency of each design (measured by rate of spin) tested. Initially the children work in the classroom, but the testing is to be completed outside under the eye of an ancillary worker. Since this school is sited in an Educational Priority Area (EPA) – that is, poor housing and social conditions locally mean that a significant proportion of the children in the catchment area are disadvantaged – two ancillary workers are appointed to assist teachers in the school, sharing their time between the various year-groups according to need.

Group 3 has a very difficult task. In front of them they have two maps. One is of Cornham in 1968, and one of the same village in 1799. Their task is to look for changes in the village over this period, and to try to account for them on the basis of things they have learned in class about village development. We can eavesdrop on their conversation as they get started:

Jane	It looks as though there's a road missing there [*1799*], because on this one [*1968*] there's a road there.
Sandra	It should be there. [*Points*]
Roy	But on that one there's only two.
Sandra	It doesn't go the same way.
Tim	I think the farmland's changed 'cos there isn't so much on this one [*1968*] . . .
Sandra	Don't forget what Mrs Roberts said – round every farm then there was usually three fields.
Jane	Yes, so they could swap crops and things around . . .

While group 3 tries to analyse changes between the maps, the fourth group is pouring over a huge leather-bound volume of the Victorian age, printed in 1874. It is a book of uplifting stories for Sundays – to be read between visits to church in that era when Sunday was closely observed as the sabbath. The book belongs to an old-established Cornham family, and is lavishly illustrated with woodcuts. The pictures are of upright Victorian families of all social strata going about their daily tasks in spiritually edifying ways. It is a fascinating insight into the mind and customs of the era; and the teacher is exploiting it in order to explore the theme 'history from records at the time'. Using this contemporary source, the pupils in group 4 have to discover the differences between clothes of today and those of 100 years ago. The youngsters talk among themselves and to the teacher:

Carol	It must be autumn or winter; the clothes are very heavy.
Michael	Yes, but they wouldn't have fashions like we do.
Suzanne	No, but their materials were made by hand.
	[*Mrs Roberts arrives*]
Mrs Roberts	How would these people have got ideas for clothes of different styles?
John	They'd have gone into market, into town sometimes, and seen what other people were wearing.
Mrs Roberts	Why are the people in this picture more fashionable than those?
Tracey	She's rich.
Carol	They're on a train, going on a journey . . .

The last group is following up its Cornham visit from notes and observations made at the time by completing questions written by the teacher and handed out on a work sheet. Here are some of the questions:

1   One of the cottages in The Avenue must have been connected with the mill. How could you guess this?
2   What was the date on Forge Cottages?
3   You looked carefully at the outbuildings of the village pub. What were they once? What connection has this with the pub here in Albert Street, Hipstone?
4   What did you notice about the door of The Grange?

We have now completed a lightning tour of the tasks in progress around the classroom, and it is time to stop a moment and to take stock. We need to notice two features about this classroom straight away.

First, the pupils embarked on these tasks within 3 or 4 minutes of returning from breaktime. They did this because all the materials and equipment required for the tasks had been laid out in advance of their return by Mrs Roberts. Each group of pupils had been issued with appropriate task instructions about what to do and how to do it. Mrs Roberts has established, over the course of her time with this group, patterns of behaviour whereby the youngsters come into the classroom quietly and get on immediately without further time being wasted on admonitions to be quiet, sit down or get on. The smoothness of the transition from break to work is dependent, then, on a high degree of organizational and managerial skill by the teacher. It looks easy; but as anyone who has tried it knows, it is really a complicated business that causes headaches for most student teachers initially.

The second point to make is that these young pupils are working in ways which make considerable intellectual demands on them; they are being asked to think about Why? questions; to reason, to use evidence, to conduct experiments and to draw conclusions. No-one would suggest that one would find work of this degree of sophistication in every primary school in the country. I have used this account – of an actual lesson, although all names have been changed – to show teaching at its exemplary best. It helps in making the point which is the purpose of this chapter, namely that teaching is an incredibly busy job! We shall pursue some of these themes in more detail later; but now we can return to watch both teacher and pupils at work at Hipstone.

Let's go back to the beginning of the lesson, to the moment when Mrs Roberts received her class back from break. She had spent some of her breaktime putting out equipment, and when the bell went she was faced by thirty pupils setting about a variety of tasks simultaneously. She had to see that everyone settled down immediately, then she quickly toured the groups to field any questions or cope with queries. Next she had to decide to visit the groups again, in appropriate order, to give help here or a slight nudge there – while keeping a general eye on everyone all the while.

Mrs Roberts' lesson is a fast-moving series of decisions and actions. By contrast, we, as fly-on-the-wall observers, can watch, pause, reflect and even (by means of a tape-recorder or video) indulge in action replays!

So now that all the groups have started work we can take

a long, cool look at how dedicated these youngsters are to their tasks. As flies-on-the-wall we can move unobtrusively from group to group. If we watch each group in turn we can see how task-orientated and busy each is. To do this we will take one group at a time and observe each individual member for 30 seconds using a stopwatch to calculate how many of the 30 seconds is spent working. By adding the individual scores together (e.g. 25 seconds for pupil 1, 15 for pupil 2) and expressing this total as a percentage of observed time (number of pupils × 30 seconds) we can get a numerical measure of time-on-task.

Group 1 is still working with the harness. There are seven pupils in the group and as we watch individual pupils work for these periods out of 30 seconds; 30, 15, 22, 30, 30, 30, 30. This makes a total of 187 seconds worked out of 210 seconds observed, or 89% time-on-task. This is a busy group!

The windmill experiments are causing great excitement. All but one pupil is working feverishly on improved sail design: in all, 165 seconds worked from 180 seconds observed – 92% time-on-task.

Of all the tasks, that with the two maps is the hardest; and from time to time concentration lapses here. Nevertheless the pupils register 48% time-on-task.

Group 4's speculations about fashion are still buzzing, though it's tempting to chatter idly about today's fashions or to thumb through the source book simply looking at the pictures rather than tackling the task. But our stopwatch shows 64% time-on-task.

Finally, the group working quietly on the work sheet appears totally absorbed – 100% on task as we watch.

The teacher, of course, needs to be aware of all this although she will not have leisure to record it as we have done. She will, however, notice who is working, where noise is starting up, whether a pupil looks puzzled or unoccupied. She will react by moving in, by asking a question, or simply with a word, a look or a gesture. This is part of the pace of classroom life; where a single day can produce thousands of interpersonal exchanges between a teacher and the pupils, and where a teacher may ask one-and-a-half-million questions in a professional career. But time is running out on us, as it always does in classrooms where the daily intervals are dominated by the sound of the school bell. So we must make another round of our working groups to see how far they've progressed before the lesson ends.

Our map group, comparing modern Cornham with Cornham in 1799, has struggled a bit, even with periodic help from the teacher. Part of the teacher's job during the lesson has been to listen to the pupils as they speculate, and by now she knows that she will have to help them to understand the maps more effectively next time. She knows, too, that the problem comes down to this: they cannot translate what they know from their Cornham visit to be large landscape features to tiny symbols on an ordnance survey map. Thus, they keep looking for the bridge, a feature of the village, on the map. But they cannot find this because they think it should be several centimetres long; after all, bridges are big. It is shown on the map simply as the river running below the road. Also, the maps are quite detailed, and the youngsters get distracted. Thus, they spend a lot of time worrying about a small stream, the course of which has been diverted, rather than concentrating on the major features of rivers and roads. Mrs Roberts' role is to monitor these problems and to reconstitute the task next time so that pupils' conceptualization of real features into the cartographic symbols is sufficiently improved to smooth out the task. So it is not only the pupils who are learning, but the teacher who has to learn from any misjudgements, to modify and to reconstruct. Meanwhile she intervenes to try to stimulate their learning:

Teacher Have you tried putting the two maps together – what's the first thing you notice?
Tracey There are more houses now.
Teacher You've answered your own question! What else have you spotted?
Roy More roads.

10

Sandra	Fields are bigger.
Alan	The river's changed.
Teacher	How?
Tim	It's straightened.
Jane	There are more trees in 1968 than in 1799.
Teacher	Yes, and that's important. The colours on the map give that away. Why should that be?
Sandra	They hold the soil together.
Tim	They look good.
Teacher	Yes – it prevents erosion. And where are they planted?
Sandra	They're mostly round the manor house.
Teacher	So who might have planted them there?
Roy	The lord of the manor.
Teacher	And who was living there 100 years ago?
Jane	Simon Ross Hammond . . .
Teacher	If the people who lived there in 1799 had put more trees there, would it have helped them? [*No response*] Well, how did they farm?
Nicola	In small fields.
Teacher	So how would it have helped them? . . .

By contrast, two groups have progressed steadily and with minimal support. Those writing up their Cornham visit with the aid of the work sheet have produced neat and accurate accounts of what they saw, which demonstrate that they observed and noted effectively. They have coped, too, with the questions which asked them to deduce and make connections between several pieces of knowledge. The windpower scientists have been equally busy. At the end of the lesson they come back, wind-blown themselves, to show their creations and comment on their efficiency. Wider sails catch more wind than narrow ones; it's best to turn the sails into the wind; small numbers of widely spaced sails are less effective than larger, more densely packed ones; stiffer card works better when the wind blows hard. Some flimsy sails have been demolished!

The fashion specialists have deduced a mine of information from their leather volume: about the nature of materials, about handmade clothing, about the toughness of materials, about limitations in colour and style. They have compared dress through the social classes and speculated about having servants to do dressmaking. Now they have been given some genuine Victorian clothes by Mrs Roberts so that they can test out their ideas; and yes, as each tries on a coat they comment on the weight, thickness, coarseness and dullness of the garment. They're about to draw and annotate some pictures of what best-dressed Victorians might have worn in Cornham 100 years ago to add to their topic folders.

Meanwhile, the puzzle of the horse's harness has been progressing for a long while, with elaborate layings out of sections and with pupils trying to simulate being the horse so as to try on the harness to test their theories. To help them in their task Mrs Roberts exploits the layout of the classroom. Basically a square, the main teaching area has a small annexe about 3 metres square. This has been blocked by a cardboard screen decorated in Dr Who fashion as a time-machine. When pupils have an old-time or historical problem to solve they can go in there to aid concentration. The harness group are now transported back in time, although it's all still a mystery. Then one astute young man has a brainwave. He sets off to look at the classroom displays, where windmills of all kinds, farm layouts and reference books are laid out to capture attention and enthusiasm. Among the exhibits he finds treasure: a Matchbox toy model of a horse and plough! With this as the model the group makes short work of the task and is praised for its resourcefulness.

Immediately before the lunch bell goes, Mrs Roberts organizes the groups for the afternoon: a change of activity and a change of pace, though still with a rural flavour. Now it's to be the story of Mr Badger. But while Mrs Roberts takes a break we can spend a few more minutes reflecting on what we have seen and heard.

What we have witnessed is a busy lesson, with the teacher controlling five different tasks, inside and outside the classroom, for thirty pupils. She has kept an eye on discipline, managed material resources, provided workcards and sets of instructions, and monitored pupil progress. Every so often she has intervened to correct, control or direct learning into appropriate channels; but she has done so in a self-disciplined way that has provoked pupils to think and question rather than to be passive recipients of information.

It doesn't take much imagination to see that an immense amount of preparation has gone into this lesson and the series of lessons to which it belongs. Mrs Roberts has done her own homework by visiting Cornham, previewing the sites of interest, working over the census records, making links with the local area of Hipstone. She has gathered stimulus materials into the classroom for display and reference. With the pupils' help she has constructed the time-machine. She has gathered together stories and support materials around the village and countryside theme. Above all, she has taken immense pains to have exciting aids to learning available in the classroom – in the present lesson a harness, old maps, a Victorian book and items of Victorian clothing. All this adds up to a considerable catalogue of work that goes beyond her 'teaching' duties between 9 am and 4 pm. Lessons like these do not create themselves, they are forged out of the ingenuity of the teacher.

The success of this lesson begins with the quality of preparation that has gone into it; but it doesn't end there. The youngsters in this class have been trained to work in specific ways. Work is group-based; the potential distraction is high, but as we have seen there is little evidence of it. This is because Mrs Roberts has helped these youngsters to achieve a degree of independence in learning which is almost unique in my experience among 8-year-olds. Pupils know where and how to find information, the questions to ask of texts and of themselves, and how to organize their time. Most impressive is the way, within each group, pupils can chat on-task among themselves. In practice, individual pupils often acted as group leaders, recalling the members to the job-in-hand when they were tempted to stray away. It was common to hear such remarks as:

(*Pupil 1 to pupil 2*) 'If you look at the workcard, Sally, we're supposed to be looking at the river. Let's talk about the houses later.'

Also underlying this lesson we can detect certain educational beliefs. It is not fortuitous that these youngsters are constantly challenged by questions, nor that they are asked to reason and experiment. On the contrary, Mrs Roberts believes that education, even for very young children, is about building a conceptual map of the world. These pupils do not learn by rote. If they deal with census figures, they don't just memorize a few salient facts; the size of the population, causes of death, some occupations. They are led into making links. Over time the population of Cornham changes: in what direction, by how much, for what cause? Do similar things happen in other villages? What does this tell us about jobs in agriculture? What other changes were happening in society at the time? Who became the important people in the population? Why were they important? What did they do for their communities? What effect did their existence have, for example, on farming methods, the landscape?

Naturally, 8–year–olds answer questions at an 8–year–old level. Be that as it may, this group of youngsters is more sophisticated and curious about the world in which it lives than many adults are.

Finally, this philosophy and approach to education has been built up into a curriculum for the children; a plan of knowledge content, of skills and of concepts which pupils need to learn over a phased period of time. This lesson on Cornham fits into a sequence which deals with villages, which in turn is part of a study of man the cultivator, which in turn is part of a study of Man.

Many of these issues are discussed in more detail as we progress through the book. For the moment it is enough to recognize that the individual lesson which runs smoothly along in the classroom is not the result of chance, not just the teacher's intuitive flair, not even a matter of one-off inspiration. The effective lesson, by the effective teacher, is the result of a battery of awarenesses, skills and flexible decisions made on the basis of sound preparation and a clearly articulated philosophy of what education is about.

In the next chapter we explore in more depth the question: What is education? For the present my aim has been to inspire you to see effective teaching as a worthwhile occupation that can, and will, absorb all the creative energy that you can muster. To do this I have relayed to you the work of one of the best teachers I have met. I make no apologies for this: only the best is worthy of emulation.

2

What is Education?

Having secreted ourselves in a classroom in Chapter 1 in order to look at the process of teaching, what we might call 'education in action', we turn our attention in the next few chapters to reflect on the question: What is education about?

To tackle this question we could approach the issue in a number of ways. Some writers, for example, have tried to produce definitions. B. F. Skinner offered the following pithy suggestion:

> Education is what survives when what has been learned has been forgotten.

In a more light-hearted view we could see what writers of both fact and fiction tell us about schools and schoolmasters, about learning and teaching. But such an approach is not very systematic.

Instead, I have selected a third course. If you had entered a college of education or, as a subject graduate, had enrolled for a 1-year course of teacher training at a university in the 1960s and early 1970s the word 'education' would have featured prominently on your timetable. In all probability this subject would then have been sub-divided into three or four strands. The traditional 'disciplines' of education are *philosophy*, *sociology* and *psychology*. In most training courses there was also a large element of the *history* of education. My own view is that, for someone coming new to the subject

16

education, quite a good overview can be achieved by looking at it in turn through the eyes of the historian, the philosopher, the sociologist and the psychologist. With these four perspectives separately grasped we can begin to piece together a more complete picture of an area of knowledge now firmly established as an academic subject in its own right.

In the first of these exploratory chapters I shall begin with the historian's perspective on education, and then go on to look at that of the|psychologist in chapters 3 and 4. In chapter 5 we will come to grips with a newer perspective, that of the sociologist. Finally, in chapter 6 a more philosophical approach to values in education is outlined. In practice what are important are the links between individual disciplines as well as their particular insights; but to separate the strands initially is probably a good way to begin. Each perspective on education asks its own distinctive questions about it. For the historian a central question is: How did education evolve into its present form? This is the question to which we shall address ourselves in the brief account of education in Britain which follows.

While the traditional universities trace their origins back to medieval days, and many civilizations and cultures have valued education for at least an element of the population, widespread compulsory education in Britain began only in 1870. But if the history of modern education-for-all began here, we need to open the story much further back in time to understand the context of educational development thoroughly.

All the great civilizations of the world (India, China, Greece) have evolved formal education systems. Often these systems were aimed only at the children of the ruling classes, who in turn would succeed to leadership roles within society. Such a practice can be seen as having sinister elitist undertones of retention of power by the few, since knowledge can be seen as power in this sense. But it is equally realistic to see such education as vocational preparation. Children of all strata in society would have been taught basic skills at home: usually craft skills and such fundamental abilities as counting. Relatively few people in very ancient times needed to write or read; universal literacy is the obsession of a highly organized society. As far as Britain is concerned, the first real contacts with more formal education may have come to pass with the Roman invasion of 43 AD which resulted in 300 years of occupation. Certainly, the Romans had schools, and the practice was doubtless imported. Children of the most important Roman families would have had private tutors. But it was in quite another way that the Romans laid the foundations of education in Britain, for they brought with them the Christian faith. Initially Christianity was an outlawed faith; but in 325 the Emperor Cosntantine gave Christianity a licence to practise and his imperial blessing. Over the next few centuries Christianity spread and though the Romans withdrew from Britain in the fourth century AD, the new religion was well established. The Saxon era which followed saw an invasion of a different kind, of Celtic and Continental missionaries. It was to these missionaries that we owe the birth of education in a formal sense, and their work was to be influential for over 1000 years.

Typical of this early period is the story of Augustine in Canterbury. Augustine came to England in 597, converted the King to the new faith, and was allowed to set up his see or bishopric at Canterbury. A little later, in 631, the early historian Bede tells us:

> The king of East Anglia was Sigebert, a good and religious man, who sometime before had received baptism while in exile in Gaul. On his return . . . he instituted a school in which boys might be taught grammar. In this enterprise he was assisted by Bishop Felix, who came to him from Kent and brought with him ushers and teachers after the fashion of the Canterbury folk.[1]

In other words, this is indirect evidence that from Canterbury onwards wherever bishoprics and cathedral churches were established there would have been schools annexed to them. Such schools concentrated on literacy and religious music. The masters were clergy and the schools provided a pool of boys who sang the services and would go on to be clergy themselves. The Church used such schools to play a major role in civilizing the people, but also to spread its teaching. Education in such schools was for a minority, however, In this way there grew up an inevitable connection between the clergy as the main educated class and powerful secular roles that demanded to be filled by intellectually capable men. From the beginning the Church established itself at the centre not only of intellectual life but of secular and political power.

This last trend was exacerbated by the rise of the ancient universities. During the period after the Norman Invasion the cathedral grammar schools tended to become absorbed into seats of learning which were, effectively, theological faculties of universities. The old grammar schools became feeder-schools for those faculties. In an age where theology was regarded as queen of the sciences this seemed quite natural. Entrants to the universities could not proceed directly to study theology; they had first to study the liberal arts and usually to become Masters of Arts before being admitted to the higher faculty. The arts were sevenfold, an idea that goes back to the ancient Greek philosopher Plato: grammar, rhetoric, logic, arithmetic, geometry, astronomy and music. The language of education was Latin. A whole succession of our ancient grammar schools was founded in this pre-Reformation period. From 1249 the Oxford colleges began to be established, for example; 1348 saw the founding at Cambridge of Gonville and Caius College and of Pembroke College. Scotland acquired a university, St Andrew's, in 1411. As time went on anyone who aspired to an academic career was almost forced to take holy orders; equally, any niche in society at large which required an educated man to occupy it was almost certain to be filled by a clergyman. The overwhelming influence of this connection between the Church and education continued into the twentieth century. As Bindoff put it: 'The Church was indeed not one profession but the gateway to all professions.'

Two historical events had far-reaching influence on the course of education in Britain, the Renaissance and the

Reformation. The former played up the role of the Greek language and literature, alongside Latin, in schools; and the invention of printing produced a greater reliance on texts rather than on oral teaching. By contrast, the closing of chantries at the Reformation cut off the supply of funds for schools; so many disappeared. Though Tudor monarchs are credited with founding many schools, in practice these were usually financed by wealthy individuals who named their foundations after the monarch out of deference or tact!

The curriculum of the Tudor grammar schools was strongly orientated towards a knowledge of Latin grammar and literature. Pupils translated verse and prose; Cicero, Virgil and Ovid were favoured authors. The remaining time was spent on arithmetic, declamation and biblical studies, but these were minority studies. A good deal of time was, however, devoted to learning the catechism and thus acquiring a sound grasp of the tenets of Christian belief. Schools emphasized good manners; and games were played to keep pupils fit. Some school foundations laid down qualifications required in the master, a BA or MA degree and fluency in Greek and Latin. Usually the master was expected to be a man of religious conviction and to live a sober life. School hours were long, starting perhaps at 6 am; corporal punishment was savage; and holidays were usually saints' days or other religious observances.

The seventeenth and eighteenth centuries brought about a change in the way people in general thought about education. Typical of one strand of development that was to have considerable influence later was the establishment of Christ's Hospital. Destitute children were removed here from the streets. Here both girls and boys received food or lodging as well as instruction in elementary reading and writing. Now, too, the foundations were laid of many of our modern Public (i.e. private) Schools to cater for those children of the aristocracy who did not have private tutors. Furthermore, as a result of the Restoration of the Roman Catholic faith to Britain, many non-conformist and Protestant teachers found themselves expelled from the traditional grammar schools and they established academies where a curriculum more directed to daily life started to be developed. Pupils might now be exposed to mathematical and scientific equipment in lessons, and may have studied French, Spanish, Italian, history, geography and politics, book-keeping and drawing. But the picture was not all progressive. As the Industrial Revolution gathered momentum social conditions, and with them school education, deteriorated. Universities, too, were experiencing a lean period. Thus a poem of the time, a parody of Gray's Elegy, describes professors who never lectured and lazy Fellows at Oxford:

> Oft have they basked along the sunny walls,
> Oft have the benches bow'd beneath their weight:
> How jocund are their looks when dinner calls!
> How smoke the cutlets on their crowded plates![2]

This deterioration in educational standards and opportunities began to be viewed critically. In the early 1800s Liberals and Conservatives clashed over the value of contemporary education. Thus it was left to the nineteenth century to effect the greatest revolution in education since the advent of the Christian missionaries in the sixth and seventh centuries. What the debates and subsequent developments of this period did was to take the power and prerogatives in education away from the Church and to put them into the hands of politicians. In a very real sense, therefore, our summary of the history of education is moving into modern times. It was one particular feature of the Industrial Revolution, the railway, that enabled the middle classes – now becoming aware that education gave their children opportunities to compete with those of more aristocratic origins in a society that needed more and more literate personnel – to send their sons quickly and cheaply to school even over considerable distances. Many famous private schools were established at this time, including the City of London, Liverpool College, Cheltenham College, Marlborough College, Rossall, and Malvern School. As a result of this new interest in schooling the Government set up the Clarendon Commission in 1861 to enquire into funding and curriculum at a number of famous Public Schools. There was a storm of protest, and the recommendations of the Commission were not widely adopted; but it had helped to throw a spotlight on secondary education in general. For the first time, too, public opinion began now to ask pertinent questions about education for girls and about the relevance of much curriculum. A Schools Inquiry Commission worked from 1864-8 on the kinds of issues raised, and recommended widespread reform. In 1870 came the Education Act which set up locally elected School Boards. These could compel school attendance of all children up to age 13. Though fees were payable, these could be waived for children of poor parents (it was as late as 1918 that school fees were abolished in all elementary schools).

Alongside improved education in this period went a demand for, and the realization of, a wider franchise. This right to vote and participate in political matters itself created a pressure for improved education of the voters. So from thenceforth it was in the interests of politicians rather than of clerics to seek progress and reform for education. The history of education from this time onwards is largely one of Government intervention, Government Reports and of centrally controlled change.

The Elementary Education Act of 1870 was a milestone. It laid the foundation of compulsory education for all; though it laid upon School Boards the discretion only to implement this. It did not do away with voluntary schools, but supplemented and incorporated them. It limited school fees to 9d a week and made provision for those who could not afford them. Individual School Boards, too, made progress. The London Board appointed school architects in the late 1800s. In 1885 the Leeds School Board opened one of the first Higher Grade Schools to cater for the new demand to 'stay on' beyond compulsory school age. Leeds also pioneered kindergartens and appointed a medical officer. So we reach a point where potentially a national system of elementary education might lead on, through the traditional grammar schools, all the way to a university career. This route was not as yet open to all, and the educational opportunities of the poorest members of society were very limited, but herein was the foundation of the twentieth-century education system.

Since the continuing story of the historical development of education is best viewed through the Acts and Reports that have emanated from Government initiatives, a glance at some of these, along with a few major events, will make up the rest of this brief historical review.

The Bryce Commission of 1895 recommended the establishment of a Board of Education to oversee both elementary and secondary education nationally. This was effected in 1899 by an Act of Parliament. Bryce also proposed that local education authorities (LEAs) be established, and this was finally achieved through the 1902 Education Act, under the guidance of Sir Robert Morant. In this way our modern LEA system, each authority having its own local education committee, was born. The old Board Schools became council schools, while many voluntary schools continued to co-exist. School managers, too, were established at this time. The 1902 Education Act, through provision of scholarships, brought closer still the reality of all-through education to university level for those who showed themselves sufficiently able.

If the Education Act of 1902 had a fault it was to view elementary and secondary education as two almost separate entities and by no means all pupils proceeded beyond the elementary stage. In the period which followed, until 1944, it was secondary education which occupied most people's minds. When the LEAs began to function they initially increased the number of secondary school places available; and because Government grants were available from the Science and Art Department the curriculum of these schools tended towards the scientific. The pendulum swung back, however, and the model of the traditional grammar and Public schools was adopted. Latin occupied a central place. A distinction was drawn too sharply between secondary and technical education. However, the social welfare aspect of school begun at Christ's Hospital started to have new promise. Following the Liberal victory in the 1906 General Election, an Education (Provision of Meals) Act empowered

LEAs to feed those pupils whose schooling suffered because of hunger; parents who could not afford the cost were assisted by the LEA. Likewise 1906 saw the passing of a clause which set up the school medical service. In addition, this Act required all fee-paying schools which were grant-aided by the LEA to reserve a quarter of their admissions each year for pupils 'gaining a scholarship' by means of an attainment test.

The year 1908 saw a number of advances in the tendency to think about education in social terms. Rachel and Margaret McMillan opened their first school clinic at Bow, moving to Deptford in 1910. The former year also saw the passage of the 'Children's Charter' (in fact, the Children's Act) through Parliament, reforming the ways in which children and young people were dealt with in the Courts. Much progress was being made to regularize methods for training and giving qualified status to teachers, and a wave of graduates was entering the profession. Then came the horrors of the 1914–18 war. Both men and women were called away to war service, and less well-qualified personnel were drafted into their places in the schools. Countless able young men from the universities died as subalterns in the rifle and artillery fire of mud-filled trenches. For those who returned, salaries were poor and not uniform from one LEA to another. The Burnham Committee of 1919 attempted to put right these wrongs.

After World War I the Labour party took up the theme of elementary and secondary education as 'Two stages in one continuous process' leading to the crucial period of adolescence. Sir W. H. Hadow chaired a Consultative Committee on the issue, and published the Hadow Report in 1926. This Report was a most significant one, and still bears much upon education as we know it.

The Hadow Report recommended the use of the description 'primary' in place of 'elementary' and the reorganization of these schools into Infant and Junior Departments. It advocated secondary education for all. Those not proceeding to the grammar schools would continue to attend either at a selective central school or at a non-selective senior department (a secondary modern school) until the age of 14. The curriculum of these schools would be practical rather than academic, and it suggested the leaving age be raised in the near future to 15. Hadow also recommended the transfer of some 13-year-olds to junior technical schools. Selection tests were proposed to identify pupils suitable for each type of education at the secondary level, and these took place at 11-plus.

The foundation laid by Hadow provided a pattern of education which has persisted, at least in part, into quite recent times. Critics have questioned the fairness of intelligence testing; of selective schooling; of the psychological soundness of transfer at 11 (believing that adolescence really begins nearer the age of 13). Not all LEAs of Hadow's time were enthusiastic in trying to establish his proposed system and make it work. Perhaps reform of primary education should have been tackled before that of the secondary sector. But Hadow set a climate in which the adolescent was regarded as important, and in which crucial issues were raised about the relationships between school curriculum and the world of work. How successful the Hadow Report's proposals could have been was never tested, although a further Report, the Spens Report, investigating the nature of secondary education was published in 1938. The Depression of the 1930s was terminated by the outbreak of World War II.

When World War II got under way, then, educational provision had seen significant change since 1870. It was universal at both primary and secondary levels. Schools shouldered social responsibilities for pupils' health and welfare. The curriculum was under review. Problems raised by Hadow – for example the discrimation of 11-plus selection – were being tackled by another commitee. Its findings, known as the Norwood Report, proposed bilateral schools – a grammar and a secondary modern school combined under one head teacher. School psychologists had been appointed, and there was particular interest in the nature and measurement of intellectual abilities. Class teaching had given way somewhat to group and individual methods, particularly under the influence of such thinkers as the American, John Dewey, of whom we shall hear later. The war saw considerable disruption to education and many city children were evacuated to safer locations in the countryside.

War often provides an upsurge of religious interest. Pressure from the Church of England drew a statement of intent from the Board of Education that plans were afoot for a major change in educational provision in the post-war period. In fact, a new Education Act was passed on 4 August 1944.

The 1944 Act replaced the Board of Education with the Ministry of Education (now, the Department of Education and Science). A Minister was responsible for making sure a new, smaller number of LEAs (each under a Chief Education Officer) carried out the provisions of the Act. Education was viewed as a lifelong process in three stages: primary, secondary and further education. Education itself was directed at the 'spiritual, moral, mental and physical development of the community.'

While the 1944 Act made provision for the continued existence of voluntary schools with various levels of autonomy from the LEA, its requirements were such as to force the Churches to relinquish some of the grip they had traditionally held on the national education system. In return the Act required religious instruction and an act of worship to be a regular part of school life. This religious input was to be non-denominational, and the instruction had to be according to an agreed syllabus to be approved by the Minister – a system which continues to the present time. Rights of withdrawal were established for parents.

As a result of the Act the school-leaving age was finally raised to 15, though not until 1947; and the intention to raise it by a further year was expressed. The Act also featured the welfare aspects of school life by laying on LEAs the duty to provide playing-fields, gymnasia, swimming baths, meals (free when necessary) and medical services. It continued the break in schooling at 11-plus, without laying down the exact organization of secondary schooling incumbent on LEAs.

Following the 1944 Act, the present system of GCE 'O', 'A' and 'S' level examinations came into being. This 1944 Act stood the test of time, and much of it remains as the foundation of the contemporary education system. The initial idealism of the Act was clouded by post-war lack of finance, by a rising birth-rate and by a desperate shortage of well-qualified teachers.

By contrast with the 1940s, the 1950s and 1960s were a time of rising economic tides, the era of Harold Macmillan's premiership with its distinctive message: 'You've never had it so good'. It was true. The school population expanded; following the Crowther Report in 1959–60 there was an impetus for improved facilities for education beyond the statutory leaving age, and a massive expansion took place in teaching training. There was growing pressure for an alternative examination system to the GCE, and this resulted in the Certificate in Secondary Education (CSE) examinations, instituted in the early 1960s, which gave individual teachers wider control over curriculum, marking and teaching methods. The highest grade of CSE pass was to form an 'O'-level equivalent, but the lower levels included in the examination system for the first time many pupils in secondary modern schools. Technical education began a phase of expansion, qualifications proliferated, even the old universities had to look to setting up more modern faculties to compete with newer universities where engineering and technology were paramount. School buildings and equipment improved with the new financial climate. Two significant educational reports were published: the Newson Report (1963) on secondary education, under the title *Half Our Future*, and the Plowden Report (1966), *Children and Their Primary Schools*.

Newson put pressure on the Government to raise the school-leaving age to 16, and this change was duly made. The Report recommended the institution of more research into teaching techniques and about the effects of environmental handicap. There was a strong vocational flavour to the Report with schools urged to relieve the pressure of public exams on those pupils for whom they were

27

unsuitable, to provide more workshop and technical facilities, and to institute appropriate curriculum for older pupils to fit them for life, society and work. This Report urged the abandonment of ability grouping in favour of broad banding; and it was instrumental in improving facilities in schools for audiovisual teaching methods. All these themes were taken up and developed in the 1970s and 1980s. In particular, following Circular 10/66, secondary schooling moved towards a comprehensive system. As schools reorganized, teachers began to reconsider methods of grouping pupils. In a climate of easy social mobility, even the broad banding system was considered by some to be socially divisive, and pupils often came to be taught in undifferentiated groups of mixed ability in the early secondary years. In some areas the Community School concept gathered momentum or became fashionable for the first time, and some new school buildings were designed to enable free access to the campus by everyone for both study and leisure pursuits.

Once again the primary sector was dealt with after the secondary, but the Report from the Committee chaired by Lady Bridget Plowden was a massive work. Plowden proposed a system of Education Priority Areas where 'positive discrimination should favour schools in neighbourhoods where children are most severely handicapped by home conditions', and such schools should receive extra financial and manpower support. The work of health and social service support services should be strengthened, said the Report. 'Teachers' centres for in-service training should be established, and there should be a large expansion of nursery education and a start made as soon as possible.'

Plowden was particularly innovative in the areas of school organization and teaching methods. The Report favoured pupils spending 3 years in a 'first school', then 4 years in a 'middle school' before transfer without selection to secondary education (this change was *only* partially and inconsistently implemented). To aid transfer between schools record-keeping procedures should be improved, and teachers should be trained to cope with more than one age group of pupils with more men being persuaded to teach younger age ranges. Plowden emphasized the need for close co-operation between training colleges and schools, for improved in-service opportunities for teachers to study, and for a full use of nursery assistants and teachers' aides.

On teaching method and the whole ethos of primary education Plowden became associated with considerable and lasting innovation. Among its paragraphs were items relating to: longer timetable blocks, more flexible curriculum, projects and 'centres of interest', using the environment, discovery learning, use of audiovisual media, the integrated curriculum. Greater parental involvement, more relaxed teacher–pupil relations, and more open-plan styles of school architecture were advocated. Attention was paid to the needs of pupils with special needs such as the handicapped, and the Report even contained a short chapter on the gifted child – perhaps the only chapter which has been almost totally ignored by many LEAs.

As the 1960s gave way to the 1970s two social trends began to effect education: a lowering of the birthrate and a deteriorating national economy. The euphoria of the 1950s and 1960s was tempered by hard reality. During this period much consolidation took place to produce the contemporary education system. Since this system is reflected elsewhere in this book and has been experienced by its readers we shall not dwell on it here but pause only to consider the role of the historian. The historian, by tracing the course of events, can contribute a valuable evolutionary perspective to our knowledge of education. For example, using his data, we can discover why some areas have schools operating under the primary/junior system while in others pupils attend first and middle schools. But the nature of the discipline – in this case history – is itself evolving. Modern historians of education are perhaps less interested in global accounts of change and more interested in exploring through local records the detailed evolution of education in a special location or in preserving accounts of contemporary events to document effectively what will be tomorrow's history. But, as we have seen, even the global history of education does not operate in a vacuum. To evolve a system of education a society has to answer value questions about the nature of the education to which it aspires and to clarify its thinking about educational concepts such as authority, discipline or curriculum content. To debate these questions of value and clarification is the field of the philosopher of education but all teachers need to come to terms with them (see chapter 6).

In the same way, history operates as a sequence of events occuring within the context of a particular society which itself evolves. Thus the increasing social welfare activities in schools represent not only a value position but an attempt to meet the needs of all or some members of society – and to reflect upon this aspect of education is the role of the sociologist (see chapter 5).

The psychologist, given that certain value judgements have been made and society has set out its contextual needs for schools, seeks to explore *how* the required learning takes place in individuals and in the groups, and to examine related factors such as the nature of intelligence, methods of intelligence testing and the effect of personality on learning (see chapter 3).

To these three perspectives we now proceed in turn in the chapters that follow, beginning with the psychological.

3

Insights from Psychology

HOW CHILDREN LEARN

In the school context, a central question of education is the deceptively simple one: How do children learn? It is the educationist specializing in psychology who tackles this question on behalf of the profession. It would be a mistake to think that we know all the answers, for psychology is a very young science. But in the paragraphs that follow we look at the current state of thinking about some key issues.

The human creature is biological in nature: as with other mammals the normal young of the species are born with the potential to function effectively in a world where the five senses – and such important abilities as processing the data from those senses into thoughts and actions – are vital. But initially those senses and abilities are rudimentary and have to be developed through maturation ('a built-in tendency in all members of a species to grow and age in an ordered sequence of events') and learning experiences. In our society it is the role of parents and later of teachers to promote this process.

In newborn infants we can readily observe that sensory (feeling) and motor (movement) functions are not fully developed. For example, in a very young baby the eyes can move independently because the infant hasn't yet the full co-ordinated control of the child or adult. In fact, the eyes of young children do not focus effectively on an object moved to varying distances. Similarly, though an infant will flinch at a loud sound, it will not discriminate between similar voices belonging to different adults. Taste probably works at the same coarse levels of discrimination. Touch is of critical importance to the infant as a channel through which to explore the world even though, at this stage, it will not have control over its limbs (motor control) to use this in more than a rudimentary way. You can demonstrate this simply enough by holding out a toy to a tiny baby and watching its jerky and vaguely directional movements in response.

Infant development is very rapid. Body weight increases quickly, and part of this growth relates to the size and proportion of the head and hence of the brain. Of course, it is the brain which is the recipient of the signals from the sense organs which lead to learning. These signals are organized and ordered within the grey and white matter protected inside the bony structure of the skull (see figure 3.1).

Precisely how the brain functions is still not known in every detail. However, the complexity of that function is clear. Messages are passed from the outside world through the nerve endings via the central nervous system located in the spinal cord into the brain itself. The right-hand portion of the brain receives messages from, and sends them to, the left-hand side of the body (and vice versa). Thus damage to the left side of the brain affects the right side of the body; left-handedness means that the right side of the brain is dominant and so on. The system of sending messages through the nervous system depends in part upon electrical impulses, something which can be tested out in a laboratory. Likewise, it is thought that certain areas of brain cells control particular functions or behaviour such as personality or motor control. Studies of brain-damaged patients seem to suggest that the left hemisphere is significantly concerned with written, spoken and mathematical language skills; the right hemisphere controls spatial skills, perception, music, dance and artistic appreciation. It now seems certain that within the brain itself some message-passing is dependent upon subtle chemical changes and it may well be that some malfunctions are the result of chemical imbalances not as yet understood.

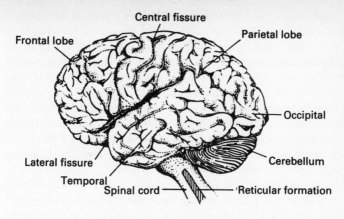

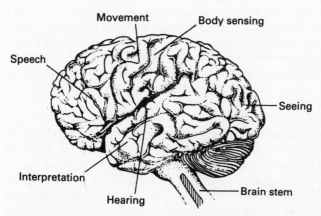

Figure 3.1 Diagrams showing the parts and functions of the brain

To function efficiently the brain needs a constant oxygen supply; hence the soundness of advice to teachers about opening a window or two in the classroom. In winter the room can be aired at breaks or lunchtimes.

The constant stream of sensory signals arriving at the brain seems to be essential to our stability. The brain stem, which links the spinal column to the brain itself, has an area called the reticular formation, where the ascending reticular activity system checks out, acts on or rejects all the signals coming into the brain from the senses. If a subject is prevented experimentally from receiving these signals he or she becomes rapidly and acutely frustrated. Among other things this experiment suggests that we need by nature to have our curiosity constantly fed through our sensory functions – an issue of considerable significance for teachers who are looking to provide interesting and provocative learning experiences for children. Wakefulness and sleep also seem to be controlled by the brain stem, and both humans and animals have a built-in mechanism referred to as a biological clock. Young children sleep more than adults and it is good pre-school routine for infants to have an afternoon nap. In the 1950s most reception classes in schools were equipped with bunks to the same end; but nowadays this is less common, and you are more likely to see 'quiet corners' where youngsters can get away from activity into more sedentary occupations as they feel the need.

As we have seen, specific areas of the brain control specific functions. To complete our brief survey we need to mention just three more.

The hypothalamus is an organ within the \ brain which controls bodily needs: hunger, thirst, temperature, aggression, sex. Obviously, disturbance or malfunction of this organ can have serious consequences. It seems to be involved in some abnormal conditions such as epilepsy.

The thalamus is an area of the brain in which fibres from the sense organs (except those of smell) meet; and its role is to sort these and send appropriate signals to motor and sensory control areas for action.

The lining to the roof of the brain is called the limbic system, and it appears among other functions to control the processing of visual cues and recent memory. Thus a child responding to simple flashcards ('sat', 'dog', 'at') while learning to read would be using these brain areas.

The outer covering of the brain is a mass of grey nerve cells, as we have seen; and specific areas appear from experimental data to be associated with specific sensory and motor functions. The front lobes are also associated with personality. It is in the grey matter that cognition or learning seems to be sited. Damage to these areas can result, for example, in speech or language problems.

The precise nature of the brain has been explored by biologists, surgeons and psychologists; but, though we understand some aspects of its workings quite well, others are a partial or complete mystery. (Perhaps one reason for this lies in the fact that educationists have, for too long, accepted the view that knowledge is sharply and clearly divided into subjects or disciplines. In fact, it is more productive to use the insights and procedures from these disciplines in a co-operative manner: research teams would be more effective if they were interdisciplinary. The same problem afflicts schools: in the primary sector pupils frequently use the methods of individual disciplines to study broad 'topics'; but at the secondary level pupils are often taught to compartmentalize knowledge into 'subjects' in preference to making connections.)

Our brief survey of the brain and its functions serves as a backdrop to the remainder of the chapter, which will deal with aspects of learning. But before pursuing this theme it is appropriate to pause in order to look at some abnormalities of brain function which might be found in children in normal schools, and which present teachers with specific problems in their daily work.

The brain is the raw material of learning and the tool through which learning functions and is expressed; if damage occurs, from whatever cause, then learning will be affected. Sometimes the process of birth is complicated and resort will be made to surgical instruments to help the child emerge. There is risk here in that, as well as direct damage to eyes or ears, the brain may undergo haemorrhage, possibly resulting in paralysis, cerebral palsy or mental defects. Sometimes the effects, though real, are slight and reveal themselves only after a lapse of time: their diagnosis can be difficult. A common birth trauma is the interruption of the baby's oxygen supply, with consequent death of brain cells. Again paralysis and speech problems may result; or the effects may be milder and subtler. Mothers are often warned against smoking or taking medication or drugs during pregnancy as the chemicals can seep through the placental barrier into the bloodstream of the unborn child and cause mental or physical damage. In holding the newborn child, care must be taken to support its head properly and to avoid impacts with hard objects. The toddler will put himself at risk: one of my own children managed, in a fleeting moment of parental distraction, to climb out of an open window and fall head first on to the concrete below – apparently without ill effects, though a child with a thin skull might have been less fortunate.

Behavioural problems of young children in the classroom are often attributed to mild brain damage of the kinds just described: though it has to be admitted that the causal connections are often unproven! Nevertheless the teacher should be alert to any information a parent may supply about birth problems relating to a particular child. At the same time, one should take comfort from the fact that the brain is very resilient. The grey matter contains more cells than we could ever need to function effectively; some research evidence suggests that the brain itself finds ways to compensate, at least in part, for damage or deficiency. Children deprived in early life of normal experiences such as speech seem to 'catch up' during adolescence as part of the normal maturation process provided circumstances become favourable and stimulating. But this last observation leads us on to the next considerations for the psychologist of education: the role of heredity, and the part played by the environment in developing the potential of the individual to learn.

Biologically, a human being is produced by the uniting of a female egg with a male sperm. The minute fertilized egg contains long and complicated threads of chromosomes or chains of chemicals. The genes which contain in potential form the characteristics of each parent are specific segments of chemical along the chromosome chain: they can be seen under high-powered electron microscopes. These genes carry parental characteristics, such as eye or hair colour, and do not mingle: rather, one is dominant over the other. Thus the child of a dark-haired mother and a fair-haired father will have either dark hair or fair hair – but not mid-brown hair, nor even streaked hair (which is a function of hairdressers, not genetic engineering!).

So, the child in your class will 'take after' either mother or father with respect to any individual characteristic. But to what extent does this limit the child's potential?

The most controversial area of debate here concerns intelligence. There appear to be three limiting factors on a child's intelligence.

1 The genetically inherited equipment with which he is born (the genotype).
2 The extent to which his immediate environment allows the *inborn* characteristics to develop (the phenotype).
3 The influence of the environment on providing experiences which extend the individual (acquired characteristics).

For a moment, let us pursue this example in purely physical terms. Tommy's father is a member of the local cricket club. When he is born Tommy's genetic bias gives him the eye and hand co-ordination that contribute to his father's success as a sportsman: genotypically Tommy could be a good batsman. Tommy goes to cricket matches from an early age, picks up bats and balls, copies his father, plays with friends in his large garden – phenotypically Tommy is developing his innate potential. By chance, Tommy's parents move house, next door to a former county XI coach who takes Tommy under his wing and teaches him to bowl as well as bat, and encourages him to think analytically about the tactics of the sport. Tommy goes on to be a great all-rounder and captain of the England XI: he has not only inherited potential and developed it, but has acquired a whole new range of related but entirely new skills.

We must assume that a similar picture applies (as a broad generalization) to intelligence; though exactly what intelligence is must be explored in more detail shortly. In fact, the picture painted so far is over-simplified in a number of ways. For example, according to this simple model two parents who were relatively unintelligent could not produce a very bright child: but because our genetic make-up includes what might be called 'rogue' genes it is possible for a child not to be limited in this way. Even to discuss intelligence effectively we need to be able to measure it, and this is a complicated issue. Before intelligence can be measured it has to be defined, and it is to this issue that we must now turn.

At one level, intelligence can be seen as successful adaptation to the environment in which one finds oneself. This could be called a biological definition because it is concerned with the human creature's response to his or her context. The small child touches a stinging nettle and discovers it hurts! Intelligence is to avoid repeating the experience. The less intelligent may take several such painful experiences before the learning is complete. A child whose limbic system in the brain had been damaged would show decreased ability to distinguish visual cues, a lessening of the fear of pain and of avoidance behaviour. Intelligence in the sense of adaptation to the environment could be said to apply to plants − a buddleia seed which escapes from the garden and subsequently grows in the soil of a blocked gutter, for example, could be said to be adapting to a new environment and clearly we need a more wide-ranging definition of intelligence than this for human beings!

A second approach is to concentrate on operations or functions. So Getzels calls intelligence 'the ability to learn acts or to perform new acts that are that are functionally useful'.[1] Ancient man took a great step forward in these terms when he learned to till the ground and sow wheat crops rather than searching for food as a nomad. But many psychological experiments with animals show that they are intelligent in this sense. A blue tit can be encouraged to discover a sequence of taps to be made on coloured buttons in order to release a peanut from a feeder. Humans, too, learn in this way; perhaps you have been to the bank already today and used your cash card to extract pound notes from the dispenser!

A better definition of human intelligence must take

account of what (as far as we know) are distinctively human abilities such as abstract reasoning and language. Something of a mouthful, but all-embracing, is Stoddard's (1945) definition:

The ability to undertake activities that are characterized by difficulty, complexity, abstractness, economy, adaptiveness to a goal, social value, emergence of originals, and to maintain such activities under conditions that demand a concentration of energy and a resistance to emotional forces.[2]

Though such a definition is not universally agreed, it does contain many of the essential ingredients. Many psychologists have tried to be more precise by suggesting that intelligence can be sub-divided. These theorists usually suggest that there is a general factor ('g'), plus a series of specific abilities such as verbal skill. While the theory fits well into broad classroom phenomena – some 'bright' children are good at a range of subjects or skills while other youngsters show a particular precocious skill in, say, music – it is not substantiated by any objective criteria. This being so, testing procedures have been hampered. Many early intelligence tests were actually tests of knowledge. Since knowledge is a product of the society in which one lives these tests tended to discriminate unfairly on children removed from their cultural contexts – for example, such a test for children brought up in a Western European context would be difficult for youngsters from Africa or for aboriginal Australians, even allowing that language problems could be overcome. Testers have therefore sought 'culture-free tests', based perhaps on abstract figures rather than knowledge or manipulation of language. Some intelligence tests are in fact not one test but a battery of tests, each of which provides a score in its own right as well as contributing to a global score. Such a test is the Wechsler Intelligence Scale for Children (Revised Version) – WISCR – which is commonly used by educational psychologists in this country. The test provides a numerical score, adjusted for age, and this is called an Intelligence Quotient or IQ.

The normal distribution of intelligence in the population on such a test is shown as figure 3.2. If one looks at the figure one can see that most of the population clusters around the 'norm' or average score; the further one moves from this norm the less frequent among the population will be people with these higher or lower scores. In the classroom simpler intelligence tests can be used and scored by teachers themselves, and teachers commonly use attainment tests, i.e. tests of knowledge, also to measure pupils' abilities. All these tests are useful guides; but their limitations should be borne in mind. The issue of the *extent* to which environmental factors inhibit develop or extend opportunity is discussed again in chapter 5. For the moment one must conclude that a child comes to school with innate potential which it is the teacher's role to develop. Putting this basic fact alongside what we have learned about maturation we can move on to look briefly at a key psychological theory of great educational significance: stage theory.

Although there are a great number of theories about how learning develops the work of the psychologist Jean Piaget (1896–1980) is the most influential on British educational thought and practice.[3] It is, in effect, a theory about how concepts are formed, and although Piaget himself was not concerned to apply the theory to classroom practice, many of his followers have done so. The few paragraphs that follow summarize Piaget's views, but inevitably simplify them.

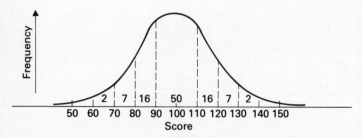

Figure 3.2 The normal distribution of intelligence

Piaget's theory has genetic roots in that it sees cognitive development as having its first stirrings in a baby's response to its surroundings. Thus, for example, in seeking the mother's nipples, an infant develops a sequence of arm movement, grasping and lifting to the mouth – a sequence that will be accommodated to secure other objects that come within reach. So the child is adapting to its environment by using a store of past actions and modifying its behaviour. These physical actions are stored and internalized. The origin of thought, therefore, lies in these internalized actions. Later, language or symbols will replace or take over from the need to work directly from the physical responses: the child will carry out the physical action in imagination (Piaget calls this an 'operation'). This ability underlies conceptual development, which itself appears to unfold in a series of recognizable steps or stages.

The sensori-motor stage (0–2 years) takes the child through the employment of reflex actions, the adaptation of these to a variety of purposes, their combination into more complex skills, to the point where emerging language enables the child to represent objects in their absence; thus building blocks become castles. So imaginative play is important in stimulating and developing these abilities which form the basis of thinking.

From 2 to 4 years approximately the child passes through what Piaget labels the preconceptual stage. The landscape in my home area is dominated by a vast cathedral. A child being driven along an undulating road towards the city remarked casually: 'Look, the cathedral is going up and down'. Thus, at this stage, the child cannot use deductive reasoning effectively; that is, use a simple rule to transfer to a specific situation. Nor can he or she use inductive reason, which involves abstracting the characteristics of situations to discover accurate rules or generalizations. This age range is characterized by symbolic play, for example with dolls, and by imitation, although the child cannot yet view the world from another individual's standpoint: he or she is egocentric.

The intuitive stage (4–7 years) spans the early years of formal schooling. At this time the child tends to concentrate on a single aspect of a situation or problem, and his ideas are formed intuitively or impressionistically. Mark, aged 7, was playing with a puzzle board; a series of questions are listed down one side and the answers, in scrambled order, down the other. By placing a pointer on the question and another on the correct answer a light is made to flash. The device works from a torch battery through simple electric circuits.

Teacher   You've got all the answers right now, Mark. Why don't you try to work out how the board works? Have a good look at it and behind it. Have you any ideas before you start?

Mark   It's magic.,

[*Later, the teacher returned*]

Teacher   How does the board work, Mark?

Mark   I think it's magnetism.

Teacher   That's a good try, it's not quite right, though. Have another look.

[*Later, she returned*]

Teacher   Have you solved it now, Mark?

Mark   Yes. It's magic.

At this stage teachers often test to see if pupils can cope with Piaget's concept of conservation. They take a piece of plasticine and roll it into a short fat sausage. Then they turn the same plasticine into a long thin sausage. The child at this developmental stage will not realize that the identical quantity of plasticine has gone into both shapes and will make a positive decision that one shape has more plasticine in it than the other.

Between the ages of 7 and 11 the child passes through Piaget's stage of concrete operations. Though language, symbol and imagination are all developing, children of this age are still dependent to a large extent on what is visible and tactile. A primary mathematics lesson is full of real objects, blocks, rods, beads, counters and so on, so that pupils can translate 'sums' into concrete realities. Conservation skill has moved on to the point where a child can understand that $3+1+5$ is the same as $5+3+1$. Similarly the child can cope with reversal: $3 \times 4 = 12$ or $4 = {}^{12}/_3$. Conservation of number occurs before conservation of area; conservation of substance, weight and volumes occur usually in that order. Clearly, this information is of significance in devising a primary school mathematics sequence or scheme!

Beyond about 11 years the child enters the final stage of conceptual development: that of formal operations. At this stage the child can construct or understand the form of an argument without concrete materials as an aid. He or she will also proceed to put a situation to the test, to experiment, to hypothesize, to make informed guesses and try them out. This is the age at which, traditionally, children transferring to secondary education have begun to carry out systematic experiments in science.

Piaget's theory is just that: one theory. It has been criticized, for example on the grounds that it has evolved from laboratory experiments, some of which are very language-dependent. It is, as stated, very neat and compartmentalized. Reality is likely to be more blurred and the stages subject to overlapping and to confusion due to the role of environmental influences on the development of individual children. Nevertheless, Piaget's theory has been widely influential as a guide to children's mental development, and one or two classroom examples are in order here.

Let us go back to the final stage, formal operations, which coincides with the passage of the pupil from primary to secondary education in many areas. The implication of this is that secondary teachers, whatever their subject specialisms, should be encouraging youngsters to guess, hypothesize, use evidence, deduce and reach logical conclusions. These ideas have been taken on board by educational researchers with a wide variety of curriculum interests. The only compulsory school subject is Religious Education (RE). Ronald Goldman,[4] studying children's religious development, found the stage theory applicable. For example, when they were presented with moral issues from the Bible, children below about 10 years of age thought in black and white terms and believed that the wrong-doers should receive retribution in return; at about $11\frac{1}{2}$ they were more inclined to probe motives and to distribute blame between several participants in the story. For children in the primary age range, Goldman pointed out that the abstract conceptual frame-work of religion is too hard to grasp; and in the decade 1965–75 the foundations were laid for a whole new approach to RE teaching based upon themes such as 'people who help us' – themes that begin from and expand upon the immediate experience of the child.

Similar work in history by Da Silva[5] showed pupils also responding in a series of clearly defined steps towards understanding. Pupils were presented with historical material in which key conceptual words had been omitted (e.g. slump, depression). The key word was, in each case, replaced by a nonsense word which would be unrecognizable to the pupil. The pupil was then asked to define what he/she thought was meant by the nonsense word. Answers were graded into four categories: logically restricted, circumstantial, logically possible, and deductive conceptualization. Each of these stages represents a move towards Piaget's formal operational level; and the grading can be used to help the teacher examine the stage of thinking reached by the individual pupil and to judge the difficulty or otherwise of the material itself. Other researchers have tried similar experiments to probe children's understanding of science, mathematics and geography. Though the detail of the experiments suggests minor modifications, for example to Piaget's age range, the basic structure of stage theory seems to be vindicated. In practice, most teachers do work to a 'conceptual map' of where the children in their classes should – subject to age, ability and environmental circumstances – have reached. What the psychologist can do is twofold: first, to refine this intuitive understanding into a testable theory; and second to explore the phenomena surrounding the theory in more detail so that teachers can build their curricula and teaching strategies on a sound basis.

Piaget's work has had a considerable influence on the kinds of teaching which go on in schools at all ages. It has given teachers the concept of mental age around which to build curriculum materials, as we have seen. At the infant level this theory has influenced the understanding of teachers about children learning through play. From the beginning the importance of language in the formation of concepts is realized; and much concentration is on language skills from the time a child enters school. Through the junior years teachers build work around visible, audible and tangible materials and experiences. As children progress into the secondary level, teachers should look for means to track and develop progress into abstract thought. Since cognitive development is cumulative, teachers place emphasis on building skills, on tracking progress and on issues such as compensatory education for those whose social or cultural environment has retarded early mental progress. All these acts are deeply embedded into the professional consciousness of teachers; and in large measure we have Piaget to thank for this!

Let us pause now to take stock. First we have discovered that many of the insights of educational psychology are about aspects of learning. For learning to be efficient it depends upon the proper functioning of the brain, and for the teacher to understand the process he must know something of the brain's working. Second, we have seen that the result of learning is something we often label 'intelligence', and we have examined some of the issues inherent in trying to decide on a definition of intelligence, in measuring it, and in surveying factors on which it is dependent. Third, we have considered a theory of conceptual development which suggests that the full intellectual potential of a human being is the result of a clearly defined maturation progress marked by a number of observable stages. Fourth, we have reflected upon the fact that such psychological theories are taken into account by teachers in the course of their daily professional lives. The time has come to survey some other aspects of psychology which shed light upon classroom practice.

NEEDS, MOTIVATION AND PERCEPTION

When you are hungry you are prompted to raid the fridge for food, you eat as much as you want, and you are satisfied. We could represent this process thus:

Need or drive $\longrightarrow$ Activity $\longrightarrow$ Satisfaction $\longrightarrow$ Drive reduction

If you are set an essay for homework the same basic processes operate. The teacher lays down the requirement, you get to work by consulting books in a library, you discover and write down information, and then decide that you've done enough to meet the requirements and so draw the essay to a close.

One of these scenarios concerns a physical drive, the other a mental one. What they have in common is a psychological basis in the questions: what motivation is operating to produce your behaviour? Why are you so motivated? Obviously in the first case the need or drive is biological: you must eat to survive. But a school is an artificial environment, so how does motivation work here, and why? Psychologists have argued for three main theories of motivation.

In the example of hunger just quoted we come close to the first theoretical formulation for motivation: instinct. The over-riding instinct to survive leads to other instincts: to be aggressive to rivals, to seek other human society for shelter and so on. These kinds of instincts are apparently observable also in animals, and are probably *part* of the human being's animal make-up. But humans are distinct from the animal kingdom in a number of ways, as we have seen; so we need to probe deeper.

Drive and need theories take us a stage further. It is often suggested that drives work at two levels: primary drives such as hunger and thirst; and secondary drives such as the need to acquire money or to own a fast car. Many secondary drives in particular seem to have their roots in satisfying social needs, for friendship, respect, or a particular lifestyle.

A third approach is a cognitive one – that is, one that looks at the way in which children think. This cognitive theory emphasizes the person's self-awareness and desire to modify his behaviour in the light of environmental factors. How hard a child tries to complete a class project successfully will depend, then, on such factors as how he responds to the particular teacher, what impression he wants to convey to his classmates, and whether he wants to please his parents.

Whichever theory is adopted the diagram on p. 46 is a useful mental map of the motivation process; but since the theories do not directly teach us about detailed classroom behaviour we need to take a look at a model which does. Such a model is shown as figure 3.3 and is based on the work of A. H. Maslow.

Maslow tied together the theories of motivation by suggesting that needs can be placed in hierarchy. Thus, survival needs must be of paramount importance; but once survival and safety are assured the individual can seek to satisfy social needs and drives. Cognitive needs form part of the self-actualization process. They cannot be satisfied, however, unless the more fundamental needs of survival and

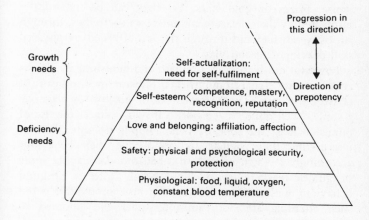

Figure 3.3 A hierarchy of basic needs (based on A. H. Maslow, *Motivation and Personality*, 2nd ed, Harper and Row, New York, 1970)

safety are met. An example of this is that our whole school system has been built up within the context that, to support classroom learning, the primary needs of children are first met through the school meals service, through the work of the School Health Service and, where necessary, by Education Welfare Officers and Social Services Departments.

Freedom from primary needs, then, allows the opportunity for the more cognitive secondary needs to be satisfied in a classroom context. But why do youngsters seek to satisfy these needs? One answer lies in the distinction between intrinsic and extrinsic motivation. Take your own case. You may be reading this book as a prelude to becoming a teacher because you are attracted by a job which seems to be reasonably secure, fairly well paid, which has good holidays and some promotion prospects, and which will allow you to select an area of the country to work in which specially appeals to you. These are extrinsic motivations. By contrast, if you have a natural affinity with children which you want to utilize, get real pleasure out of helping others and find study attractive you are intrinsically motivated. Similarly, children in classrooms can be extrinsically motivated, by praise, prizes or gold stars. Or they can be intrinsically motivated by their pleasure and interest in activities, through curiosity satisfied and through the fun afforded by physical skill development and play.

Powerful motivations are reward and punishment. Teachers constantly signal to pupils their pleasure or displeasure at classroom events. These signals can be positive or negative: a smile, 'well done', a reproof, a frown, a stare, the use of pupils' names, the tone of voice. Pupils become adept at interpreting these signals and modifying their behaviour accordingly ('Watch it! Sir's in a bad mood today!'). Some misguided teachers try to 'buy' pupils' interest or good behaviour with sweets – blatant extrinsic motivators – but such attempts are both unprofessional and doomed to failure. Physical punishment is a negative extrinsic motivator. In the past physical punishment was commonplace: caning and less severe forms of chastisement were almost a daily occurrence in schools until about the 1960s. Recently there have been moves in Parliament to restrict such violent punishment and make it subject to parental consent. In Europe generally it is now widely outlawed altogether. Both physical punishment and constant nagging or verbal reproofs by teachers seem to be of limited value: the recipients would either have reformed with milder and less consistent punishment, or else they become blasé about the punishment and it ceases to be effective.

Clearly, what a teacher must attempt is to create a climate in which intrinsic motivations take over. Ausubel[6] suggests that there is in each of us a cognitive drive which is task-oriented and which acts as a motivator in our curiosity and desire to know. Further, we are also motivated, as Maslow suggested, by needs of self-enhancement and of approval by others. The teacher must therefore set challenges to feed these springs of motivation. In the process the tasks set must be such that all children can achieve and measure their own achievement. If you have ever experienced repeated failure or too easy success you will know that both have the effect of making you lower your aspirations. It is for this reason that teachers must become skilled setters of classroom tasks and those tasks must relate to the needs of individual children.

Motivation, then, is an important psychological precondition of learning, and motivation is one of the factors which influences pupil attention in the classroom. Psychologists often explore the themes of attention and perception side-by-side as the two are inter-related, and this is the method we shall adopt here.

We discovered earlier in the chapter how the brain receives many different stimuli transferred from our senses through the nervous system. A very simple picture to illustrate this is to imagine the brain as a tape-recorder, and the senses as a bank of microphones picking up signals from the outside world. The signals are not of equal strength, and some demand more instant attention than others (compare the simultaneous awareness of the hoot of a fast-approaching car and of the lazy hum of a bee in a flower). To interpret these signals and produce appropriate

49

action some psychologists, such as Broadbent,[7] have suggested that our brains have a filter mechanism to alert us to the more pressing or unusual signals. Teachers translate these psychological insights into teaching behaviour, for example by putting eye-catching displays on classroom walls or by varying the pitch and tone of their voices so as not to drift into the background of the pupils' consciousness. Similarly a teacher with a single strategy for communication – often 'chalk-and-talk' – captures less attention and interest than one who uses a variety of presentation techniques – lecture, discussion, film, problem-solving and educational visits. These strategies are sometimes seen by the general public as 'gimmicks', but nothing could be further from the truth. Nor are they particularly 'new-fangled' since good practice has, for decades, pursued these ends. Even within chalk-and-talk lessons you will have noticed that teachers give verbal cues that alert the pupils' attention: 'Watch carefully now', 'This is important . . ., 'There are three main reasons . . .'.

Attention, or lack of it, depends too upon internal factors and psychological experiments again have important messages for teachers. A child who is hungry, thirsty or deprived of fresh air will not attend effectively: hence the need for breaks, tuck-shops and consciousness of open windows in the classroom. Attention in lessons falls off noticeably in the run-up to lunchtime. You may recall from your own schooldays how rainy breaks and lunchtimes make for fractious lessons because they conspire to deprive the pupils of the immediate physical need satisfaction and of the rests from concentration that we all need. Concentration span is an especially important consideration when dealing with mixed-ability classes, since less able children have very short spans and can be inordinately demanding of the teacher's time and attention.

But even when pupils are paying attention the way in which any two pupils will perceive a piece of teaching may vary markedly. To verify this statement simply look at figure 3.4. Each item there can be interpreted in two ways: yet the chances are that in each case only one will be

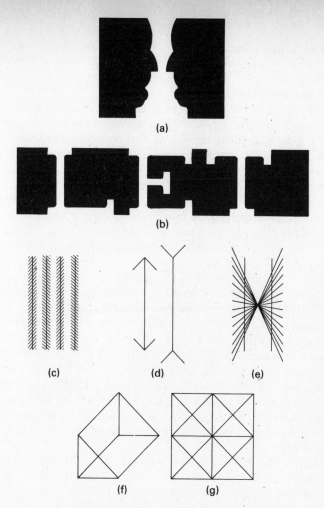

Figure 3.4 Some tests of perception

(a) can be seen either as two faces looking inwards in profile, or as a candlestick; (b) may be seen as random blocks or as the word LEFT; in (c) parallel lines are made to appear to converge or diverge; in (d) the straight lines are of equal length, but the arrows make one appear longer than the other; in (e) the two vertical lines are parallel; the Witkin test involves the subject in tracing the shape in (f) by drawing over the corresponding lines in (g).

51

immediately obvious to you. The more theoretical considerations about perception need not detain us in this brief
review: the point has been made. But several issues for the
teacher are worth noting.

Psychologists believe that how we perceive things depends
upon our previous experience; so teachers must take account
of pupils' individual social and environmental experiences.
Since individual perceptions are likely to be 'biased' in the
ways described, teachers should present learning materials
around one topic or theme in several different ways so as to
encourage pupils to build up rounded pictures of events. The
psychology of perception also tends to suggest that teachers
should not simply 'give pupils all the answers', for example
in long strings of blackboard notes or handouts, but that
they should always leave some part of understanding of the
task for the completion of the pupil himself. Many school
subjects depend heavily on pupils' abilities to perceive things
accurately and according to particular conventions; for
example, map work in geography or the accurate observation of scientific phenomena occurring during an experiment. If soundly taught from an early age such skills will be
initiated by beginning from where the pupil is, through
mapping the classroom or the school premises or from
growing cress on the window ledge and watching the results
systematically. Subsequently, more complex applications of
the behaviour, applied also to new circumstances, will be
pursued.

Given that the pupil is motivated, attends carefully and
perceives accurately what he is being asked to learn, the
information, skill or concept will pass into his memory for
later use. Psychologists do not fully understand the mechanisms by which memory works, but they do put forward a
number of theories or concepts. It is possible to think of
memory in terms of an information processing model,
where a stimulus produces a sensory reaction which is then
retained as an 'image' in the memory. (This is rather like
staring at a bright headlamp: the image burns itself into the
eye for some time after the approaching car has gone.)
Psychologists view the stored image as being retained in

either a short-term memory or a long-term memory. The short-term memory might be activated in school by reciting the six times table; repeated recitation or revision may shift the information into the long-term memory. Things which are unusual or make a large impact on the senses are more likely to be filed in the long-term memory from which the individual can carry out detailed recall after considerable lapses of time. Similarly, acquisition or memorizing is more likely to take place if conditions are favourable; that is, when a task has meaning for the doer and is carried out in a place free of distraction, in moderate bursts with short breaks, and when the learner is untroubled by personal problems. Much school work is about committing things to memory but individual pupils vary greatly in study habits at home. For instance, some work more effectively with a background radio, others without; but a lack of positive distraction and a sound psychological climate are always desirable. Once again there are lessons for the teacher from these psychological bases: about teacher–pupil and pupil–pupil relationships, about variety of teaching methods, about specific skills and techniques, about the value of revision and so on.

Teaching and learning are both expressed in language and language is so flexible that it can express the simplest thought to the most complex, and can convey all our emotions. Since it is so essential to human social life and caring we must spend a little space considering it in the classroom context.

A newborn infant can make sounds: cries or coos. By about 6 months it begins to babble. One view, held by the behaviourist psychologist B. F. Skinner,[8] is that these babbling sounds are conditioned or reinforced by reward (or need-gratification) into language. So this new language is an imitative facility for language acquisition which is refined and extended as a result of social approval or its lack. This view accounts for the (albeit limited) success of attempts to encourage chimpanzees to speak.

By contrast, Chomsky[9] believed that there is an innate facility called the language acquisition device which enables children to process incoming linguistic signals in order to produce a response: hence many language rules seem to come quite naturally to children without specific instruction. This language acquisition device (like long- and short-term memory) is not as far as we know an objective organ or specific space in the brain that can be isolated – though it may turn out to be so. It is a hypothetical phenomenon used to account for behaviour which is observed but which cannot otherwise be explained. In practice, a full psychology of language acquisition probably involves elements of both those views, and other factors, too. What can be more effectively achieved by psychologists is to observe, record and document the processes of language development. Thus we can discover that an average child will have a vocabulary of 200–300 words at 2 years old; but by 6 this will have extended to over 2500 words. Word growth is slow during Piaget's sensori-motor stage of development; but at the pre-operational stage vocabulary growth rises steeply. Language and thought or cognition do not necessarily progress simultaneously, as another notable psychologist of language, Vygotsky,[10] pointed out: in other words, a child can acquire words without necessarily grasping meaning. This whole theme is explored again in the next two chapters.

Finally in this review of the psychologist's contribution to education we need to turn to one of the underlying issues in education, but a very important one. Personality is one of the backgrounds against which learning takes place. The personality of both teacher and learner are of significance. To close the chapter, therefore, we shall explore briefly some theories of personality and also examine their educational implications.

The best-known worker in the field of personality is, of course, Sigmund Freud,[11] whose technical descriptions have even passed into everyday parlance (the ego, the Oedipus complex). Freud looked to early childhood experience and unconscious motivation as the keys to understanding the personalities of well individuals and the personality disorders of sick ones. He thought that both the subconscious and the unconscious mind were storehouses of experience that shaped personality and, in particular, that unpleasant experiences were repressed or excluded from the conscious level. These unconscious motives for behaviour arose, he thought, from defence mechanisms which protect the self from conflict or from unpalatable situations. Much of the source of this repressed behaviour Freud then traced back to childhood, and especially to unfolding sexuality. Some of these defence mechanisms are commonly observed in both children and adults. An adolescent who reverts to childish talk following the birth of a baby brother or sister is showing regression; a child who walks around dressed as an admired hero is exhibiting identification; one who fails to complete homework 'because too much reading spoils the sight' is attempting rationalization. When such 'normal' reactions get out of proportion they become neuroses and may give rise to symptoms of obsession or phobia.

Freudian theory has been developed by disciples such as Adler and Jung[12]; but the Freudian view is not universally accepted. More recently Hans Eysenck[13] has spent a lifetime researching the characteristics of personality and has suggested that personality is organized into three basic types. Each type is itself characterized by a set of behaviours which can be placed for any individual somewhere on a continuum between two extremes, thus:

Extroversion	———————	Introversion
Neuroticism	———————	Stability
Psychoticism	———————	Normality

Each person can be measured by means of an inventory of statements to which positive or negative responses are given. The respondent can then be scored to a particular point on the continuum for each of the three dimensions of the model. In America, Raymond Cattell[14] has taken this kind of thinking a stage further. His model includes sixteen personality factors which again can be explored using a personality inventory or questionnaire completed by the individual subject.

Humanistic psychology (the study of the whole person in his or her context) is less happy about exploring personality through inventories and uses as its data the detailed study of an individual's total behaviour. We have already come across one member of this school of thought, A. H. Maslow, whose hierarchy of needs was discussed on page 47. Maslow thought personality developed as the individual found a path through these needs, with the stunting of personality occurring where need fulfilment was denied. Carl Rogers applied this principle to teaching–learning situations, and emphasized the importance of the self-concept of the learner.[15] Self-concept is the degree to which an individual values himself and views himself positively in relation to peers. Psychologists have now established beyond doubt that low self-concept hinders educational progress and vice versa; so the image which the pupil in the classroom has of himself is critical to his success as a learner. Teacher behaviour such as ridiculing incorrect answers is wholly unacceptable, therefore. By contrast, those who follow Rogers welcome pupil involvement in decisions about what topics should be studied, when to move to a new topic, and about the rules and behaviour expected in the classroom.

Some attempt to reconcile these theories of personality has been made by G. A. Kelly, who put forward his Personal Construct Theory. Using a model in which a subject names individuals important in his life, and then compares triads (groups of three such persons) in which two are similar and one dissimilar, a series of 'constructs' is elicited: weak–strong, loving–hateful. The constructs help to build up (through a complicated statistical process) a picture of the subject's own personality through his perceptions of others.

However rudimentary our understanding of personality there can be little doubt that it has an important role in the quality of classroom learning and in the relationships that occur there. The bulk of research into personality and academic attainment has been done using Eysenck's measures. There are some demonstrable connections between introversion/extroversion and success. Extroverts tend to be less able to concentrate for long periods, or sustain revision for examinations. Introverts, particularly at secondary school, college or university level, gain more academic successes. Some years ago I undertook some research which involved student-teachers teaching small peer groups using the medium of discussion. Though few of the findings were statistically significant a number of trends did emerge. Thus one subject, who was measured a neurotic on two personality scales, failed almost totally to contribute (let alone lead or guide) the discussion lesson. By contrast, a very extrovert student happily dominated the proceedings even to the extent of giving false information!

Little research has been done on how teacher personality should be matched to pupils' preferred learning style. For example, we don't know if extrovert pupils do better with extrovert or introvert teachers. This is a field of discovery ripe for exploration! The most we can say at present is that teacher personality probably affects the overall style of the classroom and is a factor in deciding if it is democratic or authoritarian, teacher-directed or pupil-centred, data-orientated or problem-solving.

As we have seen, psychology does not tell us the answers to all our questions about how to make education more effective. But psychological findings and theories do shed light on, and provide food for thought about, educational processes. Psychologists in education may work in one of two major ways: studying the process of learning or studying the child who learns. In the next chapter we shall look in a bit more detail at each of these processes at work.

4

Psychology at Work in Education

In the previous chapter I described something of the nature of the discipline called psychology, and how psychology throws light on what happens in classrooms. I asked you to look at some concepts (perception, maturation, motivation) and at some theories (stage theory). In this rather shorter chapter my emphasis is on the practical application of the insights of the psychologist in just two cases. The chapter is not meant to be a rounded or exhaustive illustration of applied psychology, but simply to demonstrate some possible applications of theory to practice.

I made the point at the end of chapter 3 that the psychologist can shed light on what is taught or how (materials and methods) or on the target of the teaching (the learner). Here I shall consider an example of each.

One of the most crucial pieces of learning a child will undertake, and one which is common to all children, is learning to read. In the first part of this chapter I want to look at this subject from a psychologist's point of view, and to discuss the kinds of psychological insights which the teacher of reading needs to consider.

Piaget emphasized the importance of early environmental experience in the proper development of the child's intellect. Between the ages of 0 and 5 years the cumulative experiences of the child may have been rich and varied or relatively impoverished. Before reading can begin the teacher will need to know the child's developmental stage. It is unlikely that the teacher will undertake formal tests to establish this, but she will use professional judgements based on observation. So what will she be looking for?

The short answer to this question is: reading readiness. But this readiness might be described as a psychological state brought about by a combination of maturation (see page 31), of previous learning or through both. Though she may not consciously construe her actions in quite these ways, what she is actually doing is looking for the child's stage of development on four fronts.

1 *Environmental*. Here the teacher will observe and ask questions designed to discover the child's language background. Does he use spoken language effectively? Is it used in peer-group social situations? Only to the teacher? Is the language varied – in vocabulary, in ideas, in construction? Does he show an interest in books? Does he enjoy story-time?

2 *Psychological*. Again, the teacher will look for evidence: that the child is physically and mentally mature for his age; that he can hear accurately; that he can see, see accurately, and takes an interest in visual things; that his speech is not physically impaired in any way.

3 *Intellectual*. To be a proficient reader the teacher will want to know the child is of about average intelligence for his age; that he is normally lively and curious; that his concentration span is normal; that he can understand instructions; perhaps that he can already recognize a few words or that he memorizes stories so as (without reading ability) he can turn over the pages of a storybook at the right moments!

4 *Emotional*. In particular, the teacher will look for a stable personality, with a reasonable degree of self-confidence, and with signs of motivation.

Readiness, then, is a psychological concept which embraces a number of other psychological concepts and judgements. What the classroom teacher does is, through her professional skills, to operationalize the insights of psychology into practical decisions about teaching strategy. She has made up her mind now to proceed to teach reading to this child or

Psychology at Work in Education

group of children; she must now apply the same degree of psychological insight to her choice of teaching method.

There are two main methods in the teaching of reading. The first of these is often called the phonic method. It involves children beginning reading by learning the sounds of individual letters. When these have been mastered each consonant is then joined to each vowel sound (at, et, it, ot, ut, ta, te, ti, to, tu). Probably the next stage is to combine letters in threes to make simple words: mat, sat, cat. Thence sentences, probably rather senseless and stilted ones emerge: the cat sat on the mat. This method has the support of some behaviourist psychologists: they see direct applicability between this system and their theories of stimulus–response. In this case the letter or combination of letters, whenever it occurs, is the stimulus; the child's production of the correct sound is the response. Reading (to over-simplify!) becomes a process of marrying a whole series of letter-stimuli to sound-responses to produce words.

But the method and the theory is not without problems. For in English the rules of pronunciation are a little more complicated than this. Compare *cow*, *now*, *sow* with *tow*, *low*, *mow*: and what do you make (out of context) of *row*?

By contrast, some psychologists (the Gestalt School) recommend the 'Look and Say' approach. The thinking here is that the brain imposes patterns on the raw material of perception: it tries to turn these patterns into complete forms, for example, and to link like things. So 'Look and Say' reading schemes are built up on word patterns. Thus elephant is different from zebra. The theory is that children learn these patterns; and the words are often reinforced by pictures so that the brain can make the link between word shape and the elephant pictures. A considerable advantage of this method is that the vocabulary of simple readers can be much more exciting than that imposed by the phonic approach. The methods fails, however, to deal adequately with some of the problems overcome by the phonic approach. Thus, in shape, cat sat and mat are actually quite similar!

Since the teacher is aware, through her studies of

60

educational psychology and teaching method, of the various difficulties of teaching children to read, she will now select her method with care. Since both methods have strengths the chances are that she will adopt a particular reading scheme based on one of the methods (probably Look and Say); but it's very likely that she will also include phonic activities in her teaching as well. Children will thus approach the business of learning to read on both fronts at once. Publishers of reading schemes are at pains to point out the exclusivity of one method against another: the practical teacher is less likely to be convinced.

So the psychologist has illuminated the teacher's judgement about the readiness of children to read and has informed her choice of scheme. Some other insights from psychology may affect her practice.

First, aware that children identify powerfully at this age, she will choose the reading books in her classroom with care. So, for pupils of mixed race in a downtown suburban area, she is unlikely to choose a scheme of the kind once described as depicting 'a vanishing middle-class world in which well-dressed children play amiably with pedigree dogs in large and well-kept gardens'. Since her children will not identify readily with this world view such a scheme would simply alienate them from the taxing business of wanting to learn to read in order to enter the world of the book.

Second, she will look critically at the layout and presentation of the books she uses, and particularly at the typeface. Obviously, a style of print which accords quite closely with the children's own style of making letters will be more readily accepted by the young readers. Fussy and inappropriate typefaces may confuse the perceptions of the children that the words in the book are those they write themselves or that appear on the classroom walls.

Third, the teacher will go on telling stories and reading stories in class. To do this she will be especially aware of psychological climate. Story-time is a warm, enjoyable event – time to gather the children around you, to talk informally, to laugh, even to face frightening things together (like Roald Dahl's *The Wild Things!*). This secure climate will help encourage the will to read.

Fourth, the teacher will listen to individual children read on a daily basis. She will make a note of the children's errors, which will tend to be of certain predictable kinds: omissions, additions, repetitions, reversals and mispronunciations. She will know, for example, from psychologists' studies of eye-movements during reading and of children's perceptions of letters that children and adults do not think alike. Thus children may confuse p and b, or b and d; they do not make the 'obvious' adult distinctions of a tail above the line and one below (since the printed page, like this one, has no lines one could hardly blame a child for finding its signficance of little consequence – we as adults have learned to live with its implications even when it's invisible!). They have to learn to control exceedingly complicated eye movements over words and sentences, and in reading aloud short-term memory is brought into play so that the sense of the sentence can be compiled as it is spoken. The teacher guides the pupil into correct sequential procedures in order to interpret the symbols on the page into a spoken message.

Fifth, from time to time the teacher will want to monitor the progress of an individual pupil or of the whole class. To do this she must be familiar with one or more tests of reading skill. These tests appear in published versions and the teacher will have been trained to administer them. Some measure pupil attainment. Others are designed by psychologists to obtain diagnostic information – that is, to highlight those difficulties listed in the previous paragraph but to do so in a systematic way.

This brief review has, then, looked at the way in which a knowledge of the psychology of education can aid the teacher on a daily basis in the teaching of the material of classroom learning.

But what happens when an individual pupil shows signs of having acute problems in learning, behaviour or both?

This is the time when the teacher and the specialist educational psychologist employed by the Local Education Authority have to pool professional wisdom. Often the problems concern slow learners, and these are well illustrated in countless books on teaching remedial pupils. But sometimes pupils of average or above-average intelligence cause difficulties. The remainder of this chapter is a case study of one such child and shows the various concerned professionals working with John and with his parents to help him make more effective social and intellectual progress. The case study is reprinted, with the permission of its author Belle Wallace, from *Finding and Helping the Able Child* (by Trevor Kerry, Croom Helm 1983).

John: a case study of a child at risk

John was referred to the educational psychologist at the end of the spring term of the first year of his junior school. His teacher *recognized* his obvious ability but John was reluctant to write anything down, was inattentive yet very demanding, was overflowing with general knowledge and creative ideas but disorganised, seldom completing work or concentrating on an activity for any length of time.

He was totally rejected by the rest of the class. Firstly, this was because he appeared to them to be a very naughty boy with odd ideas they frequently failed to understand. Secondly, he was often physically aggressive: when they would not let him play, or became angry at his interference in their affairs, he would retaliate by pushing or kicking or bursting into tears. Moreover, he constantly smelled of urine, his clothes and his person were grubby and unwashed and he seemed to have a permanent cold. He was desperate to communicate and would cling to any adult who paused to listen to his monologue: the school caretaker, the domestic staff, the traffic warden, the local shopkeepers. He had developed the habit of rummaging through a number of second-hand junk shops finding odd bits of machinery and bargaining with the shopkeeper to sell them for a few pence so that he could build his inventions. He was interested in the intricacies of telephone communication so had personally sought out a senior officer at the local telephone exchange and had bombarded him with questions. The school had endeavoured to cope with him but a crisis had occurred because John was truanting regularly, missing school two or three days each week.

The teachers in John's infant school had recognized his exceptional ability and had endeavoured to provide an individualized programme of work; he had open access to all reading books which were available and staff had built up a personal library for him. Special arrangements had been made so that he could range widely and deeply in mathematics but he had always tried to avoid writing. He began to stutter because he had so much to express and was impatient even with his speed of speaking, and words would cascade in torrents. Social problems arose very early as the other children avoided him and he never had a close friend. He soiled himself as a "pay-back" mechanism whenever he felt thwarted or frustrated and his outbursts of anger stemmed from an unusual degree of determined self-will.

The educational psychologist assessed John's ability on the Weschler Intelligence Scale for children as being over 160; with a chronological age of 7:10 years, his reading age was 15+ years. The report confirmed that he was a child possessing an exceptionally high intelligence with a quality of thinking which isolated him from other children. He had particular social and emotional problems since he was naturally very affectionate and could not *understand* why other children did not like him.

Obviously John needed greater challenge and the chance to communicate and work with *intellectual* peers. His parents also needed support and guidance; they were loving, but the home was rather disorganized and John tended to live so much in a world of fantasy that basic hygiene never intruded into his preoccupation with his world of ideas.

When I met John in school for the first time, I was presented with a slight, pale, fair-haired untidy child who needed only the *slightest* encouragement to talk to me about his latest interest which was 'explosions'. He assured me that one could make a powerful bomb using cigarette tobacco, sodium and alcohol and when I asked why he was interested in explosives, from a wisdom of eight years he told me that much of the world was a junk-heap and he intended to destroy some of it and then to redesign and rebuild a more exciting world.

It seemed that the first priority was to provide John with opportunities for meaningful communication. It was inappropriate merely to present him with a series of individual 'intellectual challenges' since he was very reluctant to record, had already developed the habit of minimal written effort and was obviously very lonely. He had retreated from the real world and told everyone that he thought he had been born out of time and really belonged to the twenty-first century.

Accordingly, to ease John's sense of intellectual isolation and to

64

relieve the class teacher from his constant questioning, we decided to try to provide him with tutorial sessions when *his* ideas could provide the central theme for discussion. Contact was made with a local college which has a large science/technology department. It was hoped that one or two of the lecturers or senior students could perhaps spare an hour each week to listen to John and to guide and question his scientific theories and fantasies. John and his father were invited to the college Open Day to meet the staff informally so that they could talk to the child and possibly assess the level of his knowledge and interest. Predictably, John did not manifest himself as a studious young professor but as a rather disorganized, inattentive over-active eight year old. His attention flitted rapidly from one display to the next; when he asked questions, he appeared not to listen to the answer, he merged fact and fantasy and hardly stood still but twisted and turned, constantly scanning the large hall filled with fascinating displays.

A few days later when a meeting was held to discuss the possibility of some help for John, the college staff felt that they lacked the expertise and experience of dealing with young children, particularly in the case of a somewhat eccentric, atypical eight-year-old, and felt that although they might have the scientific and technical background, they did not have the skills of a good primary teacher.

A second approach was made to a local secondary school where one of the teachers, Mr Martin, had participated in local and countywide In-service Education courses on the 'Needs of Exceptionally Able Children'. Mr Martin had also taught on curriculum extension courses for primary pupils and so understood the problems and had personal experience in dealing with exceptionally able young pupils. Mr Martin's specialist subject was not science but we felt that perhaps he could provide John with opportunities to discuss his extensive reading, particularly in the areas of science fiction where John's appetite was insatiable and his recall of accumulated knowledge seemingly inexhaustible.

Mr Martin knew of a group of very able sixth formers who met regularly to discuss aspects of science fiction. John's dilemma was discussed with the group and a few boys offered to give up a lunch hour each week to talk with John. Their initial impression was of a child who was a careless and disorganized thinker, who was interested in everything, who talked incessantly and who desperately wanted their friendship. After several weeks Mr Martin and the students, in assessing the success of the lunch-time sessions, said that John often knew more about the latest theories in science and engineering research than they did. He asked very provocative and searching questions and, although he fantasized, his ideas were based on accurate knowledge, he merely developed them in highly original ways. He was particularly keen to apply his theories to the production of a working model and was more interested in the *functioning* than in a smart design. The students felt that they had derived more benefit from the meetings with John than perhaps John had derived from meeting them; but Mr Martin assured them that their interest, friendship and acceptance of John had helped him enormously. They might not have extended his knowledge but they had given him the opportunity to communicate and exchange ideas and had, by their questioning, encouraged him to present his thoughts coherently and logically.

An effective and real source of help and support came from Mrs Smith, a retired primary teacher who was very active in all aspects of work with exceptionally able children. In co-operation with the Headteacher and class teacher, Mrs Smith undertook to work with John on a regular weekly basis, and the following account is an extract from her report written after two terms.

I first met John at an Enrichment Day course for Juniors at our local Teachers' Centre in June 1980. At breaktimes he wandered round all the topic tables on his own. He asked me a few questions, but as the topic of 'The History of Transport since 1900 and its effect on the development of our Town' obviously did not appeal to him, he wandered off again. That which interested him most appeared to be: Byzantine chess, geology (because they were smashing rocks), and skeletal structure. All the teachers that day noted his restlessness, his constant interruptions and inability to listen.

In December 1980, the County Advisory Teacher for Gifted Children asked me if I could perhaps help John on an individual basis by going into his school once a week. The headmistress was very willing, although at first she did wonder about him getting too much attention; but at least the class teacher would be able to help the other children uninterrupted for a while.

His class teacher, very concerned and experienced, had realized John's potential and had done all she could to encourage his scientific interests, even starting a lunch-hour 'Electronics Club'. His apparent inability, or unwillingness, to concentrate on any other aspect of the school curriculum, maths, English, topics of nature, history, etc, was obvious by the poor state of his exercise books. Work was untidy, unfinished, and at about the level of an average seven-year-old. The headmistress said I could have John one whole afternoon a week and do what I liked.

My first aim was to establish a relationship, and so for the first two weeks he did nearly all the talking and I mostly listened. He. poured out words non-stop as though a dam had burst, he seemed so relieved to have a listener. Topics ranged, with startling rapidity, from lasers, repeating photography, traffic lights controlled by an individual whilst walking, Chinese language, Bristol and Brunel, volcanoes and the origins of diseases, to anagrams, palindromes, codes and ciphers, even the invention of a fairy postman who could deliver Christmas presents by remote control!

My role was to query those of his statements which seemed particularly 'way out', generally trying to find out where he had got his ideas from and why he thought it a good or bad idea. Most conversation turned to electronic devices and machines, but there was a fair sprinkling of ideas from films and television ('in 'Sapphire and Steel' they do . . .' or in 'Diamonds are Forever' James Bond did . . .') and I felt that there was much Science Fiction and fantasy mixed with his facts. John read voluminously, had a photographic memory, but (I suspect) read so quickly that he didn't always read correctly, and it was interesting to notice how adroit he was in changing the subject if (a) he did not know the answer to a question, or (b) one could prove him wrong!

At the third visit we looked at, and talked about, his class books, and I asked if he would like to make a special book with a gold card cover called 'The findings of John' – the topics to be of his choosing, but work had to be in good English and best writing. That idea did appeal, and he asked to find out about 'Fire' – we were to look up in books, jot down headings in his notebook which he would work on for the next week.

That was the *idea*, one we endeavoured to adhere to over the next three weeks, but while he had obviously glanced at some of the books, remembered one or two unusual facts, he had not done any *real* work on his topic at home or in school, although time had been allowed for it. Eventually we agreed that the first fifty minutes of the afternoon should be discussion and research, the next half-hour collating and writing in rough, and the last forty minutes used to produce a finished piece of work.

This arrangement seemed to work, there was time for some of

his ideas to come tumbling out, for us to analyze and classify them, to find the best way to express them, and at the end of the period to have produced a piece of work that was at least legible and complete. At first there was preoccupation with things that kill or destroy, special disabling bombs, killer satellites, fire machines, lasers, though he was quick to point out to me that his ioniser 'could help people with asthma and other things'. Later a short history of the area where he lived he found interesting.

When John got excited he talked very badly, taking breath in the middle of his words and gabbling, so for a few minutes each session we did some exercises in breath control. He thought this great fun, and his eventual rendering of 'Hissing Sid' showed that he *could* read poetry with expression and feeling. He has a great sense of humour, and a teasing remark often produced better work. His writing, though somewhat laboured, was quite correctly formed and written, his vocabulary was extensive, far wider than his 'creative writing' would lead one to believe.

Progress was not even, sometimes I felt I had not achieved anything, he seemed so pre-occupied, but he seemed to enjoy our sessions, was always waiting at 1.30 pm and reluctant to go at home-time.

Since going into the top junior class, he seems to have matured in several ways, he is more open to suggestions in checking his ideas and is quicker in his written work. As we only have one-hour sessions now, we have tried various games and exercises that require quick thought but careful logical answers, and then we talk of anything he has read about, seen on television, or would like to do or make. He would obviously love to haunt science and other museums, but at present they are too distant for us to visit. In the Christmas holidays, John spent nearly two hours with a friend of mine who is a Physics graduate discussing his 'gravity powered vehicle' and the friend's comment was that much of John's thinking and reasoning was 'certainly beyond O-level standard'. Hopefully in the coming year we can continue to help him so that his written skills will be commensurate with his ideas.

While trying to meet John's intellectual needs it was equally necessary to try and meet his emotional and social needs. He seemed to crave affection and physical contact. His physical appearance suggested lack of care and his enuresis exacerbated the problem of his isolation within the classroom. On one occasion he had come to school in a wet shirt because he had washed it himself that morning.

A case conference was held involving the educational psychologist, the medical officer, the school nurse, a health visitor, the class teacher, the headmistress, Mrs Smith and myself.

Subsequently, the educational psychologist interviewed John's parents and discussed their problems and his special needs. The health visitor was to visit the home regularly to help mother in organizing and coping with the demands of a very active family. Problems were discussed and the mother felt that she had some support and guidance in trying to understand and satisfy some of John's seemingly insatiable demands. Both parents undertook to listen to him more often, encouraging him to talk about his interests and ideas. They tried to manage some time to visit museums and exhibitions and he was introduced to the librarian in the local adult library so that he could borrow the books he really wanted. He began to attend school cleanly and tidily dressed responding very well to the 'gold star and chart' régime. The school nurse saw him regularly to praise and encourage and she also visited the home to provide the same support for the mother.

Since 1970, Essex Education Authority has provided opportunities for groups of exceptionally able children to work together for short periods. The courses are called 'Curriculum Extension Courses' and are seen as an essential part of an In-Service Education programme. Teachers meet regularly to explore problems of the definition and identification of exceptionally able pupils. The principles which should underlie curriculum extension and teaching methods are discussed and alternative strategies of organization explored. After the initial introductory series of workshops, teachers are invited to continue into the second stage where they prepare a curriculum extension project in co-operation with colleagues. Projects are then tried out on a curriculum extension course for pupils. This allows the teacher to evaluate the project, to gain experience of working with exceptionally able pupils and it also enables pupils to work together with their intellectual peers.

John was invited to attend a residential five-day course in the summer term of 1981. He arrived, looking unusually clean and tidy and in the very first session was immediately distinguishable by his rapid high-powered delivery of idiosyncratic fact and fantasy. The theme for the week was 'Space and Time' and so John was overjoyed to pour out his wealth of ideas. He was outstanding even in a group of exceptionally able pupils and at first reluctant to listen to the others' opinions until the teacher insisted that everyone had a right to speak and should be heard. Groups are fortunately very small to allow each child to participate fully and John began to realize that *other children could challenge his ideas and offer exciting ideas of their own*. Nevertheless, often he was functioning at a level way beyond them, leaping to a conclusion while they were still analysing the problem. He was unused to working with others and tended at first to pursue his activities regardless of other people. However, towards the end of the week, he was noticeably different, he had made friends and was especially protective of another boy who was a little shy. His greatest triumph was that two little girls actually invited him to play 'Tag'. John was also pleased because he was clean and did not smell and glowed at compliments about his appearance.

One teacher had offered to supervise unobtrusively John's personal hygiene, since he would neglect to visit the lavatory if he was engrossed in what he was doing. Even so, there were a few accidents and he needed to shower during the day and his clothes had to be washed.

After each curriculum extension course parents are given a questionnaire which invites them to comment on their child's reaction to the course. John's parents described his reaction to the course as 'ecstatic'. He talked about it constantly and they felt he was more relaxed and amenable within the family. He was so pleased to have made some friends and had gained in self-confidence and self-assurance. For the first time he had met children who had accepted him and with whom he could discuss and exchange ideas. His eyes certainly had a brighter glow by the end of the week.

John is approaching the end of his junior school phase and his headteacher feels that he is happier and better organized but, while there has been considerable alleviation, the fundamental problems of loneliness and insecurity amongst his classmates remain. His written work has improved, although his speed of thinking still outstrips his writing skills. In a report written at the end of the spring term of his fourth junior year, the headteacher wrote:

> Unfortunately, John is still prone to defiant or anti-social behaviour if he becomes frustrated. John's teachers feel threatened by this and also find it difficult to accept a feeling of personal failure even though there is reassurance that they have tried their best to meet John's needs. A common defence has been to be hyper-critical of him so that even mild deviations of behaviour which would be tolerated in other children are not considered acceptable in a child who is 'exceptionally able'.

As John approaches the secondary phase of his education, his progress will be carefully monitored. It is hoped that it will be possible to provide the individual programme he so obviously needs and that the examination success he requires to progress into higher academic fields will not be the straight-jacket is unfortunately so often is.

The story of John has helped to illustrate the complicated web of factors which go to make up the learning process and to contribute to its success or failure. Among these are social factors and issues, and it is to these social aspects of education that we turn specifically in the next chapter.

5

The Social Bases of Education

This chapter sets out to discover the nature of sociology, to see its application as sociology of education, and to examine how teachers can use its insights.

To the layman anyone who accosts him in the high street with a questionnaire on a clipboard must be a sociologist. But to understand the nature of sociology is, in reality, somewhat more complicated.

Obviously, sociologists study society. But what exactly do they study, and how do they go about the task?

One sociologist, Maurice Ginsberg, has provided four principal problems to which sociologists apply their minds and their research techniques.[1] First is social morphology, that is a study of the quantity, quality, social structure, social groups and institutions in a society. Then there is the study of law, religions, morals, fashion and other constraints that regulate behaviour; this is social control. Thirdly, there is social process or the way individuals and groups interact. Finally, the study of social maladjustment or disturbance Ginsberg labels social pathology.

W. H. Sprott, a former professor of sociology in the University of Nottingham, adopted a threefold classification.[2] He thought that sociological studies could be divided into three broad areas: studies of human social behaviour (in groups, or through values systems such as politics or religion); studies of human societies (nations, schools, villages, trade unions); and studies of Human Society (the general principles that can be deduced about the ways in which we live).

Sociology, then, is the study of society in one or more of these guises It is a relatively new subject, tracing its origin back to about 1904. It would also claim to be a scientific subject. A science is a form of knowledge that aims at objective study of phenomena or events; it sets up hypotheses that are testable; it develops objective procedures and methods for testing these hypotheses; it evolves orders and conventions for setting out its findings and for drawing and expressing conclusions. All these things the sociologist would claim to do, or at least to attempt to do. But human beings and human situations are not objective phenomena. Human researchers in social situations have to struggle to overcome their own personal values and instinctive reactions. So in some senses sociology has to work harder at objectivity than would the physical scientist, but its aspirations are identical.

For the moment, perhaps, this is enough theorizing about the nature of sociology as a discipline. The principles articulated here are probably best absorbed by looking at some examples of sociological study in action. Because this book is about teaching we shall confine ourselves to sociological studies of education, of pupils, of teachers, of schools and of school systems. The sociology of education is the subject of a vast and ever-growing literature. The method adopted in this chapter is to take just a few of the key issues in the sociology of education and to illustrate how sociologists have studied them (i.e. their methods) and what messages we are asked to draw (i.e. their conclusions). The choice of subjects and individual studies illustrated here must, because of lack of space be highly selective.

In 1984 a study was published under the title *The Social Life of Britain's Five-Year-Olds* by Osborn, Butler and Morris (Routledge and Kegan Paul). We have already established that psychologists believe that the pre-school years are highly formative, and that environment has a direct effect upon the development of human potential. Thus sociological study helps to put some flesh on the bones of the argument. For this is a book about life chances. It asks the question: what gives one child a better chance than another?

The methods used by the researchers are interesting. It is a large-scale study, but it is also a study over a period of time (the technical terms are latitudinal and longitudinal). In fact the authors followed up the first 5 years of life of the 13,135 children who were born in England, Scotland and Wales between 5 and 11 April 1970. They isolated three areas of special importance to the rising 5-year-old: the family, their pre-school education or day-care, and the employment patterns of their mothers. These areas were then studied in depth in order to build up a cumulative picture of the lives and life chances of the children studied. We can follow just a few of the strands of the research to look at the methods used and the conclusions drawn.

In the first part of the book the authors examine the families and to do this they attempt to draw up what they describe as a social index. Using insights from other sociological studies, which have demonstrated connections between factors such as social class, housing conditions, and poverty on the one hand and child development on the other, the researchers grouped together a number of variables in the family backgrounds of their sample children. These included:

● Social class (by father's occupation)
● Highest known qualification of either parent
● Type of neighbourhood
● Tenure of accommodation
● Persons per room ratio
● Availability of bathroom
● Type of accommodation
● Availability of car or van

Each of the items in the above list was given a score or weighting. We can see this at work in the measure of social class. To measure social class the Registrar General, who is the Government officer responsible for census data, uses a fivefold classification based on occupation, as shown in table 5.1.

Osborn, Butler and Morris took the five classifications from table 5.1 and scored them as follows:

Table 5.1 *The Registrar General's social classification*

Non-manual occupations		
Class I Professional	Doctor, dentist, engineer, scientist, university lecturer, etc.	A
Class II Managerial and technical	Manager, librarian, teacher, nurse, other technical occupations: pharmacist, laboratory technician, owner of small business, etc.	B
Skilled manual work		
Class III (non-manual) Clerical and minor supervisory	Clerk, commercial traveller, typist, draughtsman, policeman, secretary, shop assistant, etc.	C1
Skilled manual work		
Class III (manual) Skilled trades	Carpenter, cook, driver, electrician, fitter, hairdresser, instrument maker, painter, printer, tailor, toolmaker, etc.	C2
Semi-skilled and unskilled manual work		
Class IV Semi-skilled work	Assembler, bus conductor, farm worker, machine operator, postman, roundsman, stoker, store-keeper, waiter, etc.	D
Class V Unskilled work	Kitchen hand, labourer, messenger, office cleaner, porter, window cleaner, etc.	E

Class I	−1
II & III	0
IV	1
V	2

Similar treatment was given to the other seven items in the social index list.

Once the establishment of the index was complete a decision had to be made about how to choose the samples and collect the data. The practice is well established in large-scale studies of young children to take all those born in a specific week. This is administratively convenient since records are relatively easy to trace if confined to a single timespan. It is open to the same objections; for example, birth date tends to determine when children enter school, so those born in late July may enter school a year earlier than those born in early September. In all studies of human beings one has to accept a degree of imperfection of a magnitude unacceptable in a laboratory science. Part of the skill of the social scientist is to make sensible allowances for these imperfections.

In the present case, the children born in the 'study week' were traced through the records kept by the Registrar General's office, the National Health Service Central Register and through Family Practitioner Committees with whom all our medical records are lodged.

With the sample of children traced and identified four research documents were produced, each specially written to seek a different set of information.

The Home Interview Questionnaire. This was a set of questions of two main types commonly used in sociological research. The first involves coded responses: the sort of thing we read about in surveys as 'yes', 'no' or 'don't know' – though actually coded responses can be a bit more sophisticated than this. The second type of question is the open-ended one (e.g. How do you organize the family's budget?), where the answer must be taken down in longhand in what may turn out to be a relatively extended form. This Home Interview Questionnaire was carried out by health visitors – nurses whose special role it is to home-visit mothers with young children.

The Maternal Self-Completion Questionnaire. As its name suggests this consisted of a questionnaire of a kind that could be answered by the mother without the help, in most cases, of the interviewer. There were questions about the child's behaviour at home, about maternal depression, and about maternal attitudes to a number of relevant issues.

The Development History Schedule. This schedule was completed mainly from health records and discovered data about the child's medical record and development.

The Test Booklet. This contained assessment of the child's ability and behaviour. The tests were administered by the health visitors and included the Human Figure Drawing Test, the English Picture Vocabulary Test and Child Behaviour Scales. Some tests related to the mothers rather than to the children.

With the sample selected, the instrument for collecting the data devised and trialled in pilot experiments, and the interviewers trained (in the present case the researchers used professionally trained personnel and gave them sets of specific instructions), the research was under way.

From the data collected it proved possible to build up 'case studies' of individual families. These cases are one standard means of recording data in sociological research. They have advantage over the rawscores, charts and statistics in that they can be used to provide an air of reality in an otherwise possibly rather barren landscape. Since case study is a key method of exploring sociological data it is worth pausing over it. In the *Social Life* research considered here there are two case studies quoted at length and exemplifying the most advantaged family as identified by the social index measure, and the least advantaged. These are now quoted by kind permission of the authors and publishers.

1 A 'most advantaged' family (Social Index score 4). In this family the study child had one sister who was older than her by two years. The parents were buying a ten-roomed detached house in a well-to-do neighbourhood where the houses were well-spaced and generally well-maintained. Multi-occupation in this neighbourhood was rare and most families had higher than average incomes. In the home there was no lack of household amenities such as bathroom, indoor lavatory or hot water supply. The family had a garden where the children could play. Domestic equipment included a washing machine, spin drier, refrigerator and telephone. The family could enjoy watching television programmes in colour. They also ran a car. The health visitor who carried out the interview with the mother was of the opinion that the standard of furniture and equipment in the home was luxurious. Both parents were in their thirties. The father had degree level qualifications and was practising as a solicitor. The mother, with education to 'O' level, had worked in an office for the previous two years for ten hours a week. This she did mainly to earn money for extras, such as savings, holidays, household appliances, luxuries and the car.

The family obtained a low, i.e. 'most advantaged' Social Index score because of the father's degree level qualifications and professional status, and because they were owner-occupiers of a house in a well-to-do neighbourhood and also ran a car. However, there were additional material advantages. For example they were buying a detached house which was larger than average, and there was no lack of amenities or equipment. The father's profession as a solicitor probably brought in a higher than average income and some fringe benefits; for example, conveyancing when they bought their present home. In addition, the mother could add to the family income by doing a secretarial job for 2½ hours a day whilst the children were at school. This, then, is the kind of situation we are describing when we refer to the 'most advantaged' families in the study, of whom there were 9.6 per cent in the sample.

Elsewhere in the same city was another family whose circumstances were in sharp contrast with those of the family we have just described.

2 A 'most disadvantaged' family (Social Index score 15). This Asian family lived in a part of the city in which houses were closely packed together, many were in poor state of repair, multi-occupation was common, and most families were likely to have had low incomes. The two parents and three children occupied privately rented furnished accommodation which was shared with another family. They had two rooms of their own, but the kitchen, bathroom, indoor lavatory, hot water supply and garden were shared. A telephone was available, however, and the family had the use of a car.

Neither parent had any educational qualifications, having left school at fifteen, and the father did unskilled manual work in a factory that made motor cycles. The mother did not go out to work herself. The opportunity for the mother to seek employment would have been severely limited, however, as the study child's two younger siblings were born within little more than two years of her own birth. The mother herself was only twenty years old when the study child was born. The family had lived in the same accommodation since the time of the study child's birth.

The family had a high, i.e. 'most disadvantaged' Social Index score, because they were living in overcrowded conditions in privately rented furnished rooms in a poor neighbourhood, and the father was an unskilled manual worker. They were, however, disadvantaged in other respects also. In particular they lacked complete independence because they were sharing accommodation with another household (in fact it might have been more than one other household). Some of the difficulties probably stemmed from the fact that the mother herself was only twenty years old when the study child was born, and she had two more children before she was even twenty-three. The father's job was likely to be low paid and insecure, so that with the heavy family responsibilities there would have been little opportunity to obtain better accommodation. The mother, with three children to care for in very stressful circumstances, would also have been unable to go out to work to supplement the family income, even had she wanted to.

It is important to say at this stage that what has been described is a typical approach to a sociological study. It becomes relevant as sociology of education because it took place on children, to explore their pre-school environments, and because the findings relate specifically to the child's potential during the process of education, as we shall see. So let us look at a summary of the major findings.

The first set of findings relates to the families of the sample of 5-year-olds and their socio-economic environment. Using the social index, families could be divided into five groups according to their relative levels of advantage or disadvantage. Disadvantage was found to rest not on any single factor, such as social class or poverty, but on a cluster of inter-related factors. As many as one in ten 5-year-olds was growing up in a family classed as maximally disadvantaged and in what the researchers described as 'a level of stress and turmoil in which it is difficult to imagine a child surviving, let alone thriving'. Similarly, one in ten 5-year-olds in the sample was living in a disrupted family – i.e. where at least one of the natural parents was absent. Mothers still did most housework, with only half the fathers helping in any way at all. As regards the Test Battery, anti-social and neurotic behaviour, lower general ability, and smaller vocabulary were associated with children of those families which came out lowest on the social index. There was also increased incidence of maternal depression among these families. Children from disrupted families seemed to be doubly disadvantaged: partly from the lack of a parent and partly from the depressed economic situation of most of these families.

79

The second set of findings from this research relates to pre-school education and day-care. We have seen from the survey of Piaget's work in the chapter on psychology that development is stage-based and that early environmental experiences are critical in helping the child to progress from one stage to another. While it is probably true that the mother–child relationship is a central one in the early stages of this process, it is also true that both middle- and working-class children need the stimulus also of peers. For middle-class children this is usually seen as the opportunity to learn social skills; but for working–class youngsters there may be more fundamental needs to be met such as that of extending language use. Despite these well-documented needs pre-school educational provision is not a statutory requirement on LEAs. Typically it consists of LEA nursery schools or classes, day nurseries, private nurseries, or playgroups. The *Social Life* study looked at the utilization of these pre-school provisions. It discovered considerable regional variations in provision; where LEAs were doing little, private enterprise flourished. But in these areas particularly, the socially disadvantaged children came from families which could not afford to participate. So fewer socially disadvantaged children were able to benefit from pre-school education – arguably the very group which had most need of it. Pre-school educational experience seemed to have some beneficial influence on conceptual maturity and five motor skills as measured by the copying Designs and EPVT tests described above.

The third cluster of findings from the *Social Life* research concerns the employment of the mothers of children in the sample: 32.7% of the mothers had a job at the time the research was conducted, but only 5.8% worked full time. Of those who did not work the commonest reason was that there was a child in the family below school age: in other words, if pre-school provision were available many mothers would probably wish to avail themselves of it in order to go to work on a full- or part-time basis. Of the women who did work, socially disadvantaged mothers were most likely to accept a low status job and to work at weekends –

measures of their pressing economic need. Financial constraint (as opposed to enjoyment, or the desire to pursue a career) bore hardest upon one-parent families and the socially disadvantaged. Such mothers often had to seek a range of *ad hoc* solutions to child-minding to allow them to pursue their occupations because LEA provision is simply not geared up to the real needs of these portions of the community. Tests of the children of working mothers showed small cognitive, and larger vocabulary disadvantages accruing to the children; and full-time maternal employment added to the risk of anti-social behaviour in the child.

Here, then, are just a selection of the findings from this massive research project. They have shown up at least some of the aspects of the life chances of these youngsters. The factors that control life chances are many and varied – the only child may have more chance of mixing with adults and so improving conceptual abilities and word skills; the child with a younger sibling may learn more effectively to share both attention and possessions. The child from a broken home may suffer a degree of poverty as well as a deprivation of parental attention compared with the child of the 'normal' family. To be born in London may give a child access to facilities for health care or education denied to one in Cumbria. So this study is a review of intricate interwoven social factors that may – even in ways still only imperfectly understood – affect a child's whole future life. Vast though this sociological study is it has been described as 'a modest raid on the frontier of our social ignorance.' So it is. But for us it has served two useful purposes: to highlight the methods and material of sociology, and to introduce us to findings of considerable significance to the teacher who receives an intake of fairly eager 5-year-olds in the reception class! Let us dwell on these for a moment.

To be effective, the reception teacher must learn the instructive lessons from this research. She will get to know each child individually, and will both make allowances and actively compensate for any deficiencies she discovers in motor skills, social behaviour or language. She will quickly discover which children have received pre-school education and will help those who have not to co-operate, share and play. She will keep an eye open for any physical disabilities, especially those that affect learning, such as imperfect hearing. Even at the school gate her advice to mothers may be invaluable in helping those who are less familiar with the education system and with what can be done in the home to encourage social, linguistic and intellectual development.

So we have discovered that children enter school with a cluster of more or less valuable environmental influences behind them, influences directly related to socio-economic circumstances. In what ways exactly do these influences operate on their education? Very specific sociological studies can illuminate the more general insights of large-scale studies. One, now classic, study was into language and social class. Highly controversial in the 1960s, the work of Basil Bernstein is now accepted, if not in detail then at least as the basis of much language teaching in teacher-training courses.[3]

Bernstein had noticed differences in language use between pupils from working-class backgrounds and those from middle-class homes. In a series of theoretical and experimental papers he tried to define and formalize these differences by confining himself to this single issue.

One of Bernstein's experiments consisted of taking groups of five boys and getting them to hold discussions among themselves about capital punishment. These discussions were tape-recorded, and the language analyzed subsequently. Measures were made of the pupils' social class. The measures, and the linguistic activities of the pupils, were then correlated.

From this, and from similar experiments, Bernstein developed a theoretical model to explain his findings. In fact, what he discovered were two codes or ways of approaching language, which were associated respectively with the working-class boys and the middle-class boys, and which remained observable even when the two groups were matched for variables such as IQ.

He concluded that working-class boys used a restricted code of language, and middle-class boys an elaborated code.

The characteristic features of the two codes are shown below.

Public language: restricted code

1. Short, grammatically simple, often unfinished sentences, a poor syntactical construction with a verbal form stressing the active mood.
2. Simple and repetitive use of conjunctions (so, then, and, because).
3. Frequent use of short commands and questions.
4. Rigid and limited use of adjectives and adverbs.
5. Infrequent use of impersonal pronouns as subjects (one, it).
6. Statements formulated as implicit questions which set up a sympathetic circularity, e.g. 'Just fancy?', 'It's only natural, isn't it?', 'I wouldn't have believed it.'
7. A statement of fact is often used as both a reason and a conclusion, or more accurately, the reason and conclusion are confounded to produce a categoric statement, e.g. 'Do as I tell you', 'Hold on tight', 'You're not going out', 'Lay off that'.
8. Individual selection from a group of idiomatic phrases will frequently be found.
9. Symbolism is of a low order of generality.
10. The individual qualification is implicit in the sentence structure, therefore it is a language of implicit meaning. It is believed that this fact determines the form of the language.

Formal language: elaborated code

1. Accurate grammatical order and syntax regulate what is said.
2. Logical modifications and stress are mediated through a grammatically complex sentence construction, especially through the use of a range of conjunctions and relative clauses.
3. Frequent use of prepositions which indicate logical relationships as well as prepositions which indicate temporal and spatial contiguity.

4. Frequent use of impersonal pronouns, 'it', 'one'.

5. A discriminative selection from a range of adjectives and adverbs.

6. Individual qualification is verbally mediated through the structure and relationships within and between sentences. That is, it is explicit.

7. Expressive symbolism conditioned by this linguistic form distributes affectual support rather than logical meaning to what is said.

8. A language use which points to the possibilities inherent in a complex conceptual hierarchy for the organizing of experience.

What Bernstein himself felt he had discovered was 'how the class system acts upon the deep structure of communication in the process of socialization.' Put more simply, the social relations a child has within his or her particular social group will produce a communication system in that child (i.e. a way of speaking) which is related to that social group and its lifestyle. Thus, he believed, at one end of the spectrum working–class children develop language structures which, relative to middle-class children have

- fewer subordinate clauses;
- less complex verbal stems;
- fewer passive verbs;
- fewer adjectives;
- fewer uncommon adjectives and verbs;
- fewer personal pronouns 'I';
- simpler syntactical structures overall.

If this is true, then at critical points in his talk, the working-class child will have fewer verbal alternatives at his disposal than a middle-class child: so this kind of language is a restricted code.

At the other end of the spectrum is the elaborated code, where verbal structures are considerably more wide-ranging. Individual children's language can be placed somewhere on the continuum:

Restricted ——————— Elaborated

But where a child's linguistic skills are placed on the continuum it is likely to depend to a significant degree on his or her social-class origins.

The significance of Bernstein's research is in its implications for education rather than in the findings themselves. For he goes on to suggest that education itself is concerned with the more cognitive and abstract levels of meaning. To cope with this the learner needs an elaborated code of language. Thus already there is, on entry to school, a mismatch between the working-class child's language need and his actual language skill. This mismatch is likely to be compounded if the teacher's own language, because it is both middle class and educative, is towards the elaborated end of the spectrum. So these working-class children are likely to make less or slower progress than, on grounds of ability, they are capable of; and the restricted language itself may colour the judgements of teachers and others in authority in assessing the educational success of the child.

Bernstein's theory has been re-examined and criticized many times in the 20 or more years since it was developed. But, whatever criticisms have been levelled, its fundamental principle has been written into much language policy in schools, and the extension of language skills is fundamental to most primary education, and to the pre-school sector, too. But Bernstein has, in passing, raised another issue: the effect of teachers' perceptions of children on the performance of those children in the classroom. To explore this we shall take a brief trip to the United States of America.

Purists may question why a piece of research which is often argued to be bad research is included in a chapter which is limited by space for the selection of examples. The answer is twofold. First, it is now both famous and infamous. Second, despite its technical shortcomings it made a point of great importance that has been pursued by others since.

The book *Pygmalion in the Classroom* by Rosenthal and Jacobson (Holt, Rinehart & Winston, 1968) has, perhaps a little unfairly, become a byword for poor research into education. The study was in fact set up to explore the 'self-fulfilling prophecy' at work in the classroom. Put simply this means: the teacher makes judgement A about a pupil and regardless of whether it is right or wrong, simply because it has been made, the judgement tends to be exemplified in the behaviour of the pupil. So Miss Smith might tell Mrs Jones that Mark is disruptive. Mrs Jones cracks down on Mark almost before he has time to breathe. Mark, otherwise undisruptive, rebels. He is now both labelled disruptive and behaves disruptively: the prophecy has fulfilled itself. It has to be said at the outset that *Pygmalion* does, as a piece of research method, leave much to be desired; but its story is still instructive.

The argument of *Pygmalion* runs as follows. In everyday life people who expect to fail and are expected to fail, do fail. In education, too (be it rats in mazes or black pupils in school) there is evidence that those believed to be failures fail, and those believed to be successful succeed. If so, then in the classroom it is crucial to know how the teacher views the pupil and consequently how the pupil views himself.

To test out the self-fulfilling prophecy in the social interactions of the classroom Rosenthal and Jacobson devised a research programme. At Oak School children were tested using the school's normal intelligence-testing procedure but also using other IQ methods. The teachers were then told that the experimenters would be able to predict troughs and highspots in the pupils' performance. The experimenters would tell the teachers, tip them off, about approaching high spots for individual pupils so that they could be prepared and act accordingly.

In fact the whole exercise was an elaborate confidence trick. It was believed by the researchers that any teacher told by the experimenters that Pupil X was about to reach a new peak of ability would suddenly 'recognize' the symptoms of this new-found ability and treat the child accordingly. In fact, the so-called 'potential bloomers' were pupils selected randomly but deliberately to include pupils of high, medium and low ability!

As a result of the alleged insights given to teachers by the experimenters the 'bloomers' apparently gained impressively. In the first-grade classes the control group of pupils gained twelve IQ points during the experimental period, the 'bloomers' 27.4 points; and in the second grade 'bloomers' gained 16.5 points to the control group's average of just seven.

The morality of a piece of research conducted in this way is open to question. Other workers have also questioned the methodology of Rosenthal and Jacobson. It seems beyond doubt that some aspects of this experiment were unsound or unacceptable. Yet, in the 5 years following this book, 240 studies of the self-fulfilling prophecy had been undertaken by researchers, and over a third of them showed results which confirmed *Pygmalion*'s!

For the teacher there are many messages from research of this kind, but the fundamental ones concern teacher perceptions and their effect, and pupil self-image. The fairness and objectiveness of the teacher is vital; so is his or her ability to use assessment techniques uncluttered by personal preference or bias. But above all, the teacher must behave to pupils in such a way as to encourage and bolster a positive self-image and must never indulge in any behaviour – ridicule, sarcasm, public humiliation of pupils – which is likely to produce negative attitudes in the pupil towards the self. So the sociologist, through large- and small-scale studies can contribute to our knowledge of classroom dynamics and practice as well as look at the more global issues and principles which underlie educational provision.

Society, of course, is itself dynamic; in other words, it is constantly changing and being moulded. Sociology, too, shifts its perspectives and even the ground of its concerns. A very contemporary issue is that of gender and sex stereotyping. Much research on this topic looks at educational opportunities and how girls and women fail, for one reason or another, to take advantage of them. Thus there are, in our society, few women scientists, and even fewer girls enter the career structures in technology. If you visit a US Air Force base in Britain, you will observe women in all ranks working on identical tasks with men; but this is not a common experience in our society.

The study on the stereotype theme selected for this chapter is not, however, about opportunities as such. It begins from the presupposition that stereotyping begins long before the career choices of secondary education. Nick May (in *Pupil Experience* by F. Schostak and T. Logan, Croom Helm 1984) looked at the infant and junior classroom. His study is similar in tone to chapters 7 and 8 of this book; that is, the material is firmly based on real happenings but they are telescoped to tell the story more succinctly. Of course, the style does not invalidate the data.

May identifies a number of classroom incidents where stereotyping does, or may all too easily, occur or where it may find roots. So, observations of children's spontaneous groups at work or at play typically find boys working or playing with boys, girls with girls. Teachers ask groups of boys, or girls, to do classroom jobs in single sex contexts: two boys go on an errand, two girls clear away.

May's observations in fact suggested that lone activities like painting attract 'mixed' groups more readily than co-operative activities, be they work or play. A pupil needing a partner tends to seek one of his or her own sex. Girls are more regularly used by teachers to do tidying up than boys are. During activities boys may actually be preferentially treated compared with girls. During play, toys tend to be sex stereotyped. Balls and skittles are more readily chosen by boys; skipping ropes by girls.

May then looked at behaviour in older primary age groups. In the dinner hall his associate observed the social groupings of 7- to 8-year-olds. May examined the resulting description of events and wondered if boy bias was really built in less to the events themselves and more into the observer's preconceptions. A group of boys is reported as disruptive: but are boys really more disruptive than girls? Boys are mentioned by name in the description twenty-eight times, girls only thirteen; is this significant?

Sex stereotypes are found to permeate the stories of 9- to 10-year-olds. Recounting an imaginary Sunday at the Clifton household, both boys and girls cast Mrs Clifton and the daughter in the breakfast-preparing role; but cast Mr Clifton and the son in the consumer role!

May reflects that in a recent interview with a student teacher she 'had asked the class to join in some activities (music and movement with 6-year-olds) which the girls appeared to enjoy enormously but the boys clearly felt justified the subsequent disruption of the lesson. In order to retain disciplinary control the student redesigned her other music and movement work, thus ceding control of its curriculum to the boys through exploitation of the girls' greater acquiescence.'

The whole question of gender and stereotype in education is a subtle and sensitive one. In one of my pieces of research I collected data about many thousands of verbal transactions in classrooms. As a side issue to the main study it became obvious that boys were more often the targets of these transactions than girls: the pattern was consistent. But the differences were never large enough to have statistical significance. What discoveries like May's have to tell us is basically to be aware and that, with our consciousness raised, professional behaviour can be modified appropriately.

For our next brief look at social issues in the classroom we keep the emphasis firmly on pupils. Very few studies have taken pupils' perceptions of classroom events as the central theme. As a part of a much wider study of class management, however, Professor Ted Wragg and Kay Wood examined pupils' appraisals of teachers in a comprehensive school (*Classroom Teaching Skills*, E. C. Wragg, Croom Helm 1984). The design of their investigation is interesting.

Wragg and Wood had studied 'first encounters' – i.e. those occasions when student-teachers or teachers meet a class for the first time. The students and teachers had been asked about their strategies for establishing themselves, and were also observed in order to discover to what extent these were put into practice. In the case of some experienced teachers in the study, Wragg and Wood then returned to the sample school and explored pupils' perceptions of these teachers using interview techniques. Before doing so, however, they explored the views of a larger sample of pupils about the kinds of teaching they liked and disliked. The pupils in this wider questionnaire study comprised 200 boys and girls, fifty in total from each of four year groups. Each pupil completed a questionnaire, thirty-two items of which were adapted from a piece of research carried out in New Zealand and explored descriptions of teacher behaviour. The items measured, on a standard five-point scale, such things as teacher interest, use of praise and specific teaching skills. This phase of the research showed that pupils prefer teachers who are understanding, firm, friendly, who quickly establish a business-like climate tempered with warmth and humour. They dislike teachers who come across as unnecessarily dominant, are aggressive or tell pupils off publicly.

Subsequently a small number of pupils in the 'first-encounter' schools were interviewed in depth about teachers or students who had been studied as part of the 'first-encounter' research.

Mr Abel's approach was liked by the pupils: they found him firm, fair and humorous. Here are some of the comments made about him by children:

> 'He likes playing tricks on people. He dropped a model of a bird-eating spider in front of me. I shrieked.'
>
> 'He's not too strict, but he can be . . . like when you break more than two lab rules in a day . . .'
>
> 'We once made a mobile. Mine was funny. It wasn't good. We both laughed at it.'

The impressions of the liked teacher accorded very precisely with both observers' accounts of his behaviour and his own descriptions of his teaching style.

In addition, the pupils were shown a photograph of a classroom incident and were asked how Mr Abel would have handled the situation. Their assessments were remarkably close to his description of what he would have done in the situation pictured.

By contrast, Mr Baker was not liked. He expressed his own assessment of his teaching tactics thus:

'I believe in confrontation. It is an attempt to maintain standards. Most people just operate for a policy of containment . . . . You have to remember that to clash with you is to clash with the school, the culture and ultimately society. If they get away with it in school then they will end up as trouble-makers in the unions . . .'

Pupils' views of Mr Baker found him more vaccilating:

'He's too strict. He says he treats us like he was taught at school. He never does anything interesting. He makes the book a lot harder . . . He goes over and over the boring bits.'

'He changes his mind.'

'If anyone laughs or talks they have to stand up for the rest of the lesson. He said, "Smile and work well and you'll be alright" . . . If I saw Mr Baker smile the next thing you would see would be a pink elephant.'

The researchers described Mr Baker's lessons as: universally negative, lacking humour and unremitting tedium. Clearly in this case, the less able teacher lacked an important skill: the ability to analyse his own behaviour while observers (be they pupils or researchers) agreed completely. So pupils do, apparently, form clear, accurate and consistent views of teachers. They do also respond to positive qualities. One message of this research is that pupils' views of classroom events might well be worthy of a more serious consideration than is generally accorded them. When you qualify yourself you might do well to be at least a little sensitive to the views of pupils about your performance.

For the final insight of sociology into the business of teaching I have selected to leave the social dynamics of classrooms and to look at teachers as a profession through the eyes of Trevor Noble and Bridget Pymm. The teaching profession itself is a fair target for sociological study; and in an article in the *British Journal of Sociology* these two investigators looked at the social background of teachers, and some of the implications of this ('Recruitment to teaching in the years of expansion', Vol. 31, No. 1, March 1980).

The underlying question of the Noble and Pymm research is: What mix of social-class origins do we find among recruits to the teaching profession? There are several reasons for asking such a question. First, access to all forms of higher education including teacher training is believed to be improved for all segments of the population: but is it? Second, we have seen how the linguistic codes of teachers may militate against effective learning by some pupils (Bernstein's theory, above); so shouldn't the profession reflect more nearly the social mix of society at large? Third, over the years between 1960 and 1975 many children of manual workers found themselves in professional jobs because these were the years of economic advance and therefore of improved social mobility: so were these trends present also in the teaching profession, which was also expanding rapidly?

Noble and Pymm selected an LEA in South Yorkshire and were given access to information about students who trained for teaching in a given period of time. In fact, there were three groups of entrants to the profession:

1 Trainees from a college of education following a 3-year certificate course between 1974 and 1977 (this course is now replaced by the BEd described in chapter 10).
2 Trainees following the (then optional) BEd degree course from 1974 to 1978.
3 Those who had followed a BA/BSc degree course plus a 1-year postgraduate certificate in education to qualify in 1978.

The entrants listed in groups 1–3 above were all assessed for social-class origin using the categories set out earlier in table 5.1. Percentages of entrants from groups 1 and 2 falling to each social class are given below. The results are compared with the previous large-scale investigation in

The Social Bases of Education

1961 taken from the Robbins report, and are shown in table 5.2.

These raw scores need some interpretation. Though the percentage of 1974/78 entrants falling to the social classes 4 and 5 had actually risen, a background knowledge of the South Yorkshire LEA suggests that the raw scores may be misleading. In fact, South Yorkshire is a community with a substantial working class population; and Noble and Pymm predicted, that to be truly representative, 56.5% of 1974/78 entrants should have come from classes 3M, 4 and 5. The actual figure was well below this at 45.6%. When the figures for group 3 entrants (degree and postgraduate certificate route) were scrutinized and compared with the 1961 figures the percentages of working-class entrants had remained stable. In other words, because recruitment to teaching had increased in 1974/78 compared with 1961, the actual *numbers* of entrants from working-class backgrounds had increased in this period; but their *proportion* of the total teaching force had either remained stable or decreased. Also, though the proportion from classes 4 and 5 had increased slightly, the proportion from class 3M has decreased substantially.

Incidentally, as far as this batch of entrants was concerned, the research revealed that 'not only do women outnumber men by two to one, they are more likely to come from middle-class families'.

Table 5.2 *Social class and teacher training*

Social class	% of entrants from training colleges (groups 1 & 2) 1974/78	% college entrants 1961
1	11.2	7.4
2	30.8	36.2
3 (non-manual)	12.4	14.9
3 (manual)	29.6	29.8
4	13.0	9.6
5	3.0	2.1

These calculations were completed at the end of a period of economic expansion when teaching, too, was an expanding profession. The pendulum has now swung the other way. It is interesting to speculate upon the legacies of this recruitment pattern for the structure of the profession in the 1990s; and also to ponder what kind of entrants will be attracted then!

In this chapter we have reviewed just six studies in the sociology of education and the social dynamics of classrooms. They have opened up some pertinent issues; but have neither explored these in adequate depth nor given a rounded picture of the sociology of education. Such investigations, do, however, help to illuminate some of the bases upon which we make decisions and form value judgments on matters educational. This is a theme to which we shall return in the next chapter, where we explore some issues and values in education.

6

Issues and Values in Education

Most of us are exposed to formal education in a State or private school from the age of 5 onwards. To that extent we tend to take education for granted, and may not seek its aims or question its nature. But in this book so far it has become clear that we can both observe the processes of teaching and learning at work, and also that we can take a detached and even theoretical look at education as a phenomenon in our society and in previous eras. Inevitably, then, we are drawn to ask: What is the purpose of education? Why is this phenomenon, so central to our existence and experience, constructed in the way it is? Perhaps, too, what alternatives are there? It is the role of the philosopher of education to debate these questions in depth. To do so he or she has traditionally studied the great theoretical thinkers of the past or present.

Thus, one of the earliest and most famous philosophers was the ancient Greek, Socrates. In a series of dialogues with various companions, documented by his pupil and admirer Plato, Socrates put forward a complete philosophical system in his *Republic*. This view recorded by Plato is sometimes labelled Idealism, though it would be less misleading to call it Idea-ism. According to this view the universe is an expression and embodiment of Mind. Our perceptions of the universe change with time and circumstance, but Mind does not change. This ultimate existence or eternal principle includes values: beauty, truth, goodness. These values are discoverable by human beings, who ought to dedicate themselves to cultivating them. Socrates went on to develop his system into a picture of the perfect State or Republic. This Republic contains features which are abhorrent to our modern minds; for example, Socrates was honest enough to believe that human beings do not have equal talents, he divided his citizens into men of gold, silver and bronze who would perform differentiated tasks in society. Perhaps for this reason more than any other Socrates is now rather out of fashion in our age of equality!

Some of Socrates' views are a long way from those of our own century. He believed, for example, that censorship was important in education. His justification sounds reasonable enough:

> Children cannot distinguish between what is allegory and what isn't, and opinions formed at that age are usually difficult to eradicate or change; it is therefore of the utmost importance that the first stories they hear shall aim at producing the right moral effect.

Socrates was clear about what was educationally sound for his own day: uplifting examples of self-control, of obedience to commanders and rulers, of religious principle, of independence. For 'the object of education is to teach us to love beauty'. Thus, he was equally clear about what was not suitable: stories of the gods engaged in immoral acts, a tendency to laugh too often, and the work of poets who portray the emotions. After all, he claimed, witnessing 'bad taste in the theatre may insensibly lead you into becoming a buffoon at home'.

Another school of philosophy is given the description Realism. This starts from the fundamentally opposite view to Idealism: whereas Idealism believes that only 'ideas' or Mind have ultimate reality, Realism asserts that only 'things' have real existence. Educators who are persuaded by this philosophy tend to reject the academic in favour of the practical in the curriculum, to value doing rather than reading. As pupils grow older, exponents of this view emphasize the vocational aspects of education – learning for the 'real' world of work and employment. This movement would also favour some modern developments in education such as the community school, where close links are fostered between pupils and the people and institutions among whom they learn. It would also approve such current educational innovations as the Youth Training Scheme (see below), where 16-year-old school leavers are given a chance to divide time between a place of employment and off-the-job skills' training in a Further Education College. Even in college the work is highly practical; and the descriptive language used reflects this emphasis – e.g. learning to use a piece of equipment is known as 'hands-on' experience.

Another well-known philosopher of the past who has effected our thinking right into the present time is Jean-Jacques Rousseau, who lived from 1712 to 1778 and whose school of thought is known as Naturalism.

Rousseau's *Emile* is a study in the upbringing of one child from birth to maturity. Perhaps the study is best understood in the light of a quotation from another of Rousseau's works, *Du Contrat Social*:

Man was born free, and everywhere he is in chains.

Thus Rousseau begins from the premise that 'nature wants children to be children before they are men'. Education is part of a natural process of maturation, then: and this accords with Rousseau's more general views of the essential goodness of nature and of human kind, who are guided to goodness by the light of conscience. It was a view at odds to a large extent with that of the contemporary Christian Church, which emphasized the doctrine of original sin; and Rousseau was effectively regarded as a heretic.

For Rousseau, the major principle of education was that it had to be child-centred. He was one of the earliest writers on education to put forward what has become known as a 'stage theory'; i.e. the view that a child passes through various stages of levels of cognitive (or intellectual) and emotional development and that learning has to be appropriate to the particular stage reached. This theory has, in one form or another, become a cornerstone of much psychological work in education, and we have mentioned it already especially in the context of Jean Piaget.

Rousseau valued liberty of the individual highly, but he also believed in 'the discipline of natural consequences'. Thus a young person could learn by experience and error, within a relatively safe context, rather than by rule and restraint. Similarly, the distinction between work and play is blurred; and there is a recurrent emphasis on 'learning by doing', which informs much of modern primary-school thinking. Rousseau put experimentation and discovery above instruction, and he urges that Emile 'not be taught science, let him discover it'.

The goal of education in *Emile* is self-realization, self-development. This view, combined with a basic belief that Nature and Society are in conflict, is perhaps inconsistent with his acceptance that a child's later education is to maintain an intelligent and effective membership of society. Rousseau was an early advocate for political education, and for education for the role of marriage partner; unlike Socrates, he even welcomed exposure to literature and drama as a way of acquiring aesthetic taste.

Among modern educators those who most closely follow Rousseau's philosophy have been A. S. Neill and Michael Duane. Neill set up a school called Summerhill. He called it a demonstration school because 'it demonstrates that freedom works'. Neill was widely criticized for his liberal approaches, which are summed up in this extract from his own work (*Summerhill*, Penguin Books 1976):

> We set out to make a school in which we should allow children freedom to be themselves. In order to do this, we had to renounce all discipline, all direction, all suggestion, all moral training, all religious instruction. We have been called brave, but it did not require courage. All we required was what we had – a complete belief in the child as a good, not an evil, being.

Neill became famous, or infamous, for allowing pupils to make decisions at a school parliament, for allowing nude bathing, and for his outspoken clashes with traditionalism. Since his school was a private one he was able to go his own way. Michael Duane, however, was headmaster of a State school, Risinghill Comprehensive, in Islington. This school, too, proved controversial and was closed in 1965.

Though most schools do not adopt such extreme philosophies there is a continuing theme in education of 'formal *vs* informal', whether it be schools or teachers. In part this divide reflects the kinds of basic philosophies described here. Something of the thinking of Rousseau even informs the Plowden Report referred to earlier. Emphasis on pre-school education, on play in early childhood, on natural development all recur in Plowden.

Many critics of Rousseau's views point out that on almost all fronts he overstated his case. On the other hand, much that appears in *Emile* is now accepted uncritically as standard educational practice. Certainly heuristic or discovery methods in science and in other fields of knowledge, are widely advocated (if not always practised!). The importance of play and of direct experiences for young children are axiomatic in nursery and infant schools. Rousseau, however heretical, was a necessary counterblast to the Church's distorted and misunderstood doctrine of original sin. Perhaps Rousseau's durability depends on the provocative nature of his ideas and the resulting use of them by other individual philosophers and schools of thought. Certainly, the link between Rousseau's ideas and those of John Dewey and the Pragmatist school will emerge as we proceed.

Dewey was an American who lived from 1859 until 1952. He was a professional philosopher, and was influenced by his studies of Pragmatist philosophers. In general tone he would have accepted the view of William James that 'True ideas are those which we can assimilate, validate, corroborate and verify. False ideas are those we cannot'.[1] This was the 'pragmatic test' for truth. Dewey had grown up in an age which, because of the impact of the theory of evolution and on account of the accelerating pace of social and scientific change, was uncertain about its traditional beliefs and values. He himself would have subscribed to the view that:

> Even scientific laws are but generalizations which may be
> modified again and again – they remain true only as long

as they summarize truly the current state of human knowledge.[2]

Another influence on Dewey was his upbringing in a close-knit New England community; and he saw education as a means to break existing social barriers and form a new society. Dewey, like Rousseau, adopted a stage theory of human development, which accorded well with his evolutionary standpoint. He thought children passed through three stages: a play stage (4–8 years), a period of spontaneous attention (8–12 years) and a stage of reflective attention (12 plus). Putting together these influences on Dewey's educational thinking we can now examine this in a little more detail.

The principles of education that Dewey advocated he also put into practice by starting an experimental school. These principles were that the natural and spontaneous activities of children can be harnessed to educational ends, that the teacher's role is precisely to harness these activities and to direct them to co-operative living, and that such education will lead children to behave in a spirit of co-operation and mutual interdependence as they proceed into adult society. For Dewey education is an empirical exploration which leads to both mental development and social integration.

For Dewey, the child should proceed to learning initially through a problem of his own devising. Because the pupil was motivated to know the answer to this problem he would begin to speculate about it. With help, the child would come to make observations and gather information about the problem. Then the pupil would begin to put together ideas, guesses or hypotheses about the problem, and would test these out.

Thus Dewey came to draw upon the child-centredness of Rousseau's theories, and to extend the idea into something that has become popularly known as 'the project method'. His name was linked to the Dalton Plan: a contractual method of education in which the pupil worked at his or her own rate on an assignment while the teacher played a consultative, as opposed to an instructional or didactic, role.

He emphasized the need to begin from the child's starting point or stage of development rather than at a level predetermined by the teacher. As we shall see later many of Dewey's ideas link a philosophical standpoint with psychological theory.

John Dewey's legacy to modern educational practice is immense, even when it is not fully acknowledged. In the last two decades there has been an increasing interest in teaching from the starting point of the environment, in drawing up teacher–pupil contracts of work, in abandoning 'subjects' for a more thematic approach, in learning through play and in experiential learning. Primary schools are particularly influenced by Dewey's ideas, which have been disseminated over the years through absorption into such documents as the Plowden Report, mentioned earlier in this chapter, and you may care to re-read chapter 1 at this point to try to trace the extent of Dewey's influence on the lesson recorded there. But even in the secondary sector the rise of the CSE examination has brought into prominence project work and special studies. Some degree courses at universities include assessment for work of this nature. Experimental approaches to learning science, such as the widely adopted Nuffield Science scheme, are precisely Deweyan in tenor.

However, it should be stressed that the traditional method of looking at the past is only one approach that the philosopher brings to his reflections upon education; the more common one nowadays is the application of techniques of modern analytical philosophy to issues and problems. The modern philosopher's role, then, is to help us to define our ideas, concepts and language more clearly and to express our thoughts more exactly. Alan Beck puts it concisely as follows:

> Philosophy, then, will take important educational concepts, such as child-centred education, the needs of the child, equality, learning by discovery, indoctrination, and so on, and it will attempt to clarify them – to show what they can legitimately mean, and to expose any muddle that may arise from the improper use of such terms or

from fallacies inherent in arguments involving such terms. Philosophy will take a long, hard look at various educational theories and attempt to point out where they may be confused, or based upon rather questionable assumptions which the theorist has failed to bring out into the light of day.[3]

Philosophy, therefore, is a reflective activity involving the identification and debate of key educational issues as they arise. In the remainder of this chapter I shall attempt to survey just some of the important educational issues of our time. It will not be possible to discuss in detail all these issues, nor to bring the full weight of philosophical analysis to illuminating them. Rather, I shall aim to take a reflective look at the kinds of questions of value and matters of concern that grassroots teachers all have to face, and to pose questions rather than suggest solutions.

A fundamental issue for all teachers in every era is: Education for what? One could offer a variety of replies, not necessarily mutually exclusive. Here are some possible suggestions:

- for citizenship
- for employment
- for sound social behaviour
- for morality
- for the improvement of the mind
- for understanding
- for knowledge
- for reason
- for freedom
- for life

This list is certainly not exclusive, but it does give a broad picture of education that would be acceptable, even *in toto*, to many people at first glance. When we begin to probe these answers in more detail, however, it may be that we would wish to define and modify our items or select among them. For example, on the face of it we would probably embrace education for citizenship as one broad general principle for education. But, for what kind of citizenship? The citizenship of a democratic State? If so, should the nature of the State change to an ultra-Left or ultra-Right regime, would this aim be abandoned? And democracies differ, so that a secular or humanist democracy cannot be equated with a Christian or a Hindu one. Clearly, then, education for citizenship needs redefinition, and as a purpose for education the teacher would need to explore its implications. For it is likely that any dozen parents would, while supporting the principle, embrace quite different concepts of its meaning and implications.

In the same way, much contemporary Government thinking discusses education in terms of employment. But many of the documents in which this view is articulated (such as the Green Paper, *Higher Education in the 1990s*)[4] fail to clarify exactly what is meant. Implicit in the document is a view of society which is almost wholly dominated by science and technology. Education in school and beyond is seen as a way of preparing young people to take part in such a society. Yet this view is open to question. While it remains true, and will continue to do so, that science, technology and information technology are likely to increase in significance in all our lives, just one implication of this is that leisure is likely to increase – workers may spend less hours at work when machines bear the workload, and unemployment may increase. Yet nothing is said of the role of education in helping to fill that leisure time productively. Then again, this same science and technology in the medical sphere keeps people alive longer and helps them to stay fitter; yet nothing is said of education for retirement, of education for social care and so on.

In much the same way, we could debate the other responses on our list. Education for sound social behaviour begs questions about the values underlying the word 'sound', and about the nature of society. Education for morality raises issues about traditional Christian values in an increasingly multiracial and multicultural community. Education for freedom asks us also to view critically the need for individuals to exercise responsibility.

So far, too, we have assumed that the context for education would be the school. But many, such as John Holt[5] or Ivan Illich[6], would suggest that school fails precisely to fit young people for any of the purposes in our list. Thus schools are less about freedom and sound social behaviour and more about unthinking social conformity; they are not about understanding, but about absorbing and trotting out accepted wisdom without the benefit of critical analysis. In fact, such de-schoolers would claim, what schools *do* teach quite often is not success but failure by stifling individuality; and they fail most notably at the very thing they rate highest – education for life and work. Thus, to put it simply, the child of an isolated agricultural family which has spent generations tilling the soil is going to learn more about life (as he or she will live it) living and working at home than by leaving the context of daily life to enter the false and contrived world of school.

The answer to the question 'What is education?' is far from being as simple as we first thought. Our analysis has raised issues and questions of value. This is a fundamental area that you will have to think through for yourself throughout your career as a teacher, revising and refining your view in the light of experience. For the moment we shall concern ourselves with just a brief selection of rather more contemporary issues for you to begin/ to contemplate.

An important issue which is exercising the minds of teachers, headteachers and administrators at present is that of falling rolls. The rate of population growth rises and falls because it is affected by external influences. For example, after World War II many husbands returned home from abroad after long absences from young war-time brides. Shortly afterwards there was a dramatic increase in the birth rate; a phenomenon which made an important impact on schools 5 years later. Similarly, in good economic times the average size of families increases, and it decreases again when times get hard and when lack of money precludes looking after children easily. Obviously, there is a delay between these factors first becoming apparent and the time when they affect schools: about 5 years to hit the infant

sector, 7 or 8 to affect the junior schools, and 11 and more to
reach secondary education.

From a school point of view, the downturn in the birth
curve over recent years because of factors such as improved
contraception, working women starting families later or not
at all, economic hardship and so on, has a detrimental effect.
Fewer young children come into the education system.
Classes may become smaller – which most would see as an
advantage. But the unit cost of providing those classes – the
number of teachers, buildings, even cleaners – remains the
same; so LEAs and Government attempt to save money by
telescoping classes. Instead of four in a year group there
might be three, thus saving the cost of a teacher; or smaller
schools may close to save running costs and overheads. So
begins a spiral of unemployment at all levels within the
profession.

When the decreasing birth cohort of children reaches the
secondary school there may be even worse implications.
Since schools receive funds using a system which takes into
account both the total number of children and their ages
(where older pupils receive more money than younger
ones), and since both the overall sums of money and the
number of senior teaching posts is dependent on this points
system, not only are jobs directly affected but so are the
promotion prospects for those teachers who remain. Figure
6.1 gives birth trends over recent years, so you can begin to
do some calculations of your own!

One critical problem of falling rolls for the secondary
sector is that, as individual teachers leave or retire, they may
not be replaced. Since most secondary teachers are subject
specialists this policy may leave crucial curriculum gaps in
the school. Sometimes an LEA will make judgements: it
may not replace a musician who leaves but may seek a
replacement physicist. The implicit value system underlying
such a decision is a live issue in education, one which could
well be addressed in the reflective philosophical way
described earlier in the chapter; but it is certainly one which
must exercise the minds of all educators, parents and pupils.

Obviously, with school rolls falling there are currently

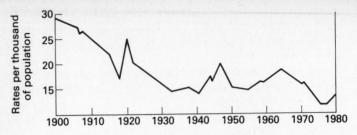

Figure 6.1 The birth rate in England and Wales 1900–80 (from
Population Trends 1, HMSO, London, 1975, p. 6 and
Annual Abstract of Statistics 1982, HMSO, London,
1982, p. 35).

more teachers available than are needed by the system. This
does not mean that newly trained teachers are failing to be
employed at all. What it does imply is that the best-qualified
young teachers stand the best chance of employment; and
since most are trained on LEA grants they are more likely to
be employed in their sponsoring county or metropolitan
borough than elsewhere. But, once in the profession, all
teachers are waiting longer for promotion. To offset this
delay unions are pressing for revised salary structures to
ensure longer scales of annual increments so that one does
not reach a pay ceiling too early in one's career.

Government statisticians watch over social data such as
birth trends with a view to predicting the number of
teachers required in the longer-term future. Their conclusions are used by the National Advisory Board (NAB),
which limits the total number of training places available for
teaching across the country and regulates the individual
intakes of each training institution. Theoretically at least,
some balance is thus achieved between supply and demand.
The falling rolls' issue, therefore, has both pros and cons. If
it raises standards among candidates for teacher training and
in those who qualify it will, indirectly, have been beneficial.
In so far as it forces out able teachers, closes educationally
effective but less economic schools, or limits curriculum
choice, it must be viewed with abhorrence.

Another issue which is almost always under active debate somewhere in the country is the organization of education. Traditionally, we have seen infant, junior and secondary sectors with transfer at 7-plus and 11-plus. But across the country it is possible to find any of the following schemes:

- zero nursery provision
- nursery classes in infant schools
- nursery units
- 5–7   infant schools
- 7–11   junior schools
- 5–8   first schools
- 8–12   middle schools
- 5–11   all-through primary schools
- 9–13   middle schools
- 14–16   secondary schools
- 11–16   secondary schools
- 11–18   grammar schools
- 11–18   comprehensive schools
- sixth-form colleges
- 16+ education in Further Education Colleges
- 18+ education in FE, HE, polytechnic and university colleges
- private education at all levels

Within the State-controlled sector of education numerous re-organizations have taken place either to amend the age of transfer or, following Circular 10/66 from the DES, to move increasingly towards a non-selective secondary scheme. These re-organizations may be hotly debated. The age of transfer debate, for example, might centre around educational issues such as appropriateness in the light of stage theory (see chapter 3); or it may have financial undertones in enabling an LEA to close some redundant buildings to save running costs. In the case of non-selective secondary education, those in favour of comprehensive schools would argue apparently factually on the basis of the inaccuracy of the 11-plus selection procedures, or philosophically that equality of opportunity implies open access at all levels of the education system. Supporters of selective State education

107

at 11-plus may be motivated politically (catching parental votes in a middle–class constituency), educationally (arguing for quality and maximizing individual opportunities to exploit talent), or pragmatically (that the high standards and proven results of a specific school should not be eroded). Obviously these summarized arguments do not exhaust the issue; but they do give a flavour of the debates, which are often emotional affairs.

Once inside a school, however it is organized on the macro level, one has a related problem to solve at the micro level: How should children be divided up into classes? Should pupils be streamed by ability? Should there be broad bands – i.e. a nine-form entry in a comprehensive school could be divided into three bands each of three classes by high, middle and low overall ability? Should there be setting – i.e. the most able mathematicians go into the top maths set, the most able at English to the top English set and so on on a subject basis? Or should there be a total mix of ability in each case? And, if so, on what basis could classes be selected – randomly, by testing to ensure a spread of ability, by friendship groups of pupils, or in some other way?

Similarly the debate about the private education sector has always been a hot potato. Private education means, in effect, that those who are rich can buy access to 'better' schools than the relatively poor who have to make use of the State system. But all sorts of questions are begged by this superficial, but common, description of the problem. For example, are private schools really 'better'? What is meant by 'better'? No doubt some prestigious ones can afford to pay teachers above the going route or provide perks such as cheap housing on the campus. In these cases they may attract more academically able men and women; but will they necessarily be better at the task of teaching what they know? Many private schools exist on quite low budgets: so instead of providing better facilities by way of laboratories and so on, they may actually provide less despite the fees which are charged. Some parents would favour a system whereby, if they were to opt out of State education which is financed through the rates paid by property owners, they could obtain credit vouchers to be exchanged at private schools to offset a proportion of the fees. But how many people would opt out, and would that number be so great as to bankrupt the State system so that it could no longer function effectively? In a democracy, indeed, is the very existence of a private option a right and reasonable facility? These are hard questions of value to which, again, teachers have to put their minds.

Once in a school, the nature of that experience will have a lasting effect upon the child. As far as learning is concerned, there are a number of models to which a young person may be subjected. In the private sector, for example, emphasis tends to be from the earliest years of the preparatory school upon academic excellence and what might be called the 'information model'. Chidren learn 'subjects'; and the choice of subjects is likely to include a modern language (usually French) from the junior years onwards. At the second stage, this model of education may still include Latin; youngsters who are able will be entered for a large cluster of 'O' levels, perhaps nine at one time and often taken a year early; and sixth-form work will have its sights clearly upon entry to Oxford or Cambridge and either the professions or direct entry to the management side of business or commerce. Teaching methods tend to be relatively formal, data-based, and associated with relatively traditional social values and norms of behaviour.

In State schools, young children may have a much more 'play-orientated' model. Working on the assumption that much early learning of both experience and information comes through play, but that many children lack this experience (because both parents work, through urban deprivation or on account of lack of opportunity to socialize in high-rise flats or rural isolation), teachers emphasize the need to work out these needs through, for example, sand and water play. In the best examples of this model, play is in fact carefully structured by the teacher to bring about learning outcomes. Many of these will be affective, that is about successful interpersonal relationships: sharing, co-operating, taking turns or making friends.

At the junior level, the child may experience the 'discovery–learning' model of education. Classroom tasks are not given closely defined boundaries by the teacher: 'copy this picture', 'write ten lines about a ginger cat'. Rather, learning is presented as a series of problems: 'suppose you were to . . .', 'what would happen if . . .?', 'why do you think . . .?'. In these cases children are guided in techniques of studying for themselves, such as using reference books and finding their way around them by means of the index or contents page. Such learning, as we have seen in this chapter, has much to do with the pioneer experiments of John Dewey, and was given a boost in the Plowden Report (see page 27).

In State schools, secondary education may follow the information model described above, or the discovery–learning model. Often the child of 11-plus finds that he is weaned on the latter and proceeds to the information model as he approaches GCE examinations. CSE examinations, by contrast, were an attempt to preserve some features of the discovery model at the 16-plus age level; success is usually dependent in part on a project completed by the child himself on some area of the subject chosen out of interest. The new GCSE examination, which may replace the other two forms in the medium term, is an attempt by the Government to introduce a new unified system of examining that will both introduce a grading system spanning GCE and CSE attainment levels, and incorporate the more flexible methods of the CSE. At the time of writing plans for the introduction of this new system of examining have ground to a virtual halt because of the pay and conditions dispute between Government, LEAs and teacher unions.

At 16 years of age the young person may enter a College of Further Education, where another 'model' of learning is prevalent: the 'vocational model'. This model assumes that learning should be fundamentally directed at equipping the learner for his or her chosen career. Practical or 'hands-on' experience is the keynote. So potential nursery assistants will do some classroom work directly related to the development of the young child, and will spend some time in nurseries, private homes, hospitals and other locations making detailed studies of young children and learning to look after them. Potential surveyors will be classroom-based to discover the necessary theory connected with the job and to familiarize themselves with the equipment they will use; then they will go out to use the equipment in real surveying tasks to test out those skills and their proficiency in them.

This last model, the vocational one, has become increasingly in favour with the Government in recent years. It seems likely that recruits to the teaching profession in the next decade will be caught up in a number of schemes that aim to bring vocational education more firmly into the secondary-school curriculum. Among these are the Certificate in Pre-Vocational Education (CPVE) and the Technical and Vocational Education Initiative (TVEI). CPVE is a curriculum which involves a common core (with ten areas as disparate as social skills and information technology), vocational studies (which relate to specific areas of employment), and additional studies (broadly aimed at the personal development of the student). The fundamental aim of CPVE is 'to assist the transition from school to adulthood by further equipping young people with the basic skills, experiences, attitudes, knowledge and personal and social competencies required for success in adult life including work'.[7]

TVEI is another Government initiative still in its trial stages and aimed at persuading young people of 14–18 years of age to seek qualifications of direct relevance to work. Schools and Further Education institutions work together to provide experience for youngsters in areas such as design and technology, catering, business studies, horticulture and so on. There is work experience, too, for the school pupil so that bridges into adult and working life are built more effectively from an earlier age.

Beyond school, many youngsters now join the Youth Training Scheme (YTS), which provides about 4 days per week of experience in a workplace plus a total of 65 days a year of classroom-based, off-the-job training. YTS is changing from a 1-year to a 2-year scheme; and it is relatively attractive because trainees are paid a small wage.

Obviously, what has been said in the preceding paragraphs about models of education and about the tendency for vocational education to be seen as all-persuasive at the Government level, raises a whole series of questions of value for educators. Indeed, the issues are fundamental: What is education? What are its purposes and objectives? What is the relationship between education for personal development and education for work? One should even ask questions about the world view which produces these vocationally orientated schemes: have the politicians, for example, got the vision of the future – on which this model is based – correct? What are the likely future needs of our young people, and how are they going to differ in fact from those of your generation or mine? What are the most effective means to satisfy these needs and to achieve the goals that have been identified?

Obviously, the cluster of issues that relate to the nature of education in a changing vocational climate cannot be exhausted in a short chapter such as this, but enough has been said to indicate the kinds of problems that a teacher will face in the coming decades. In the same way we ought to glance at the changing social climate and raise an issue or two about the difficult question of moral education. Traditionally, British schools have taught moral education largely through the medium of religious education. The 1944 Education Act, which is still in force, requires each school both to give religious instruction and to hold a daily act of worship. While the latter is widely ignored in practice, with assemblies held less regularly or turned into largely secular occasions, most schools do in fact include religious education (RE) as a curriculum element. But society is changing: in many areas of the country Christians (even nominal ones) hardly exist, and immigrants have brought to the local schools their own religious traditions, values and cultures; RE teachers have responded by adopting a more multi-faith and multicultural approach to syllabus content. But the issues remain and not only about alternative faiths but about alternative, often non-religious, value systems.

Thus there is increasing pressure for schools to include particular viewpoints or areas of study in their curricula: political education, peace studies, feminism, humanism, anti-racist studies and so on. Here is a short and very selective list of live issues about the content and approach to teaching of religious and moral education in schools today.

1 Should members of immigrant cultures (Sikhs, Muslims) be allowed to set up their own exclusive schools?
2 Should Church schools be abolished?
3 Should the protected place of RE under the 1944 Education Act be terminated?
4 Ought school assemblies no longer to include an act of worship?
5 Hasn't society grown out of religious 'myths'?
6 Has the RE slot become a 'curriculum of despair', pursuing social or political issues without real insight into them?
7 Can moral education be tested through public examinations?

Gender and race, both issues in connections with the moral education debate, are also issues in their own right. Gender issues tend to revolve about two central pivots: first, the possible differences in educational opportunity accorded to women by more or less subtle discriminatory treatment, and second the attitudes towards women held by those (men) in positions of power and influence. As regards the former it is claimed (the evidence is often strong and persuasive, but sometimes more ambiguous) that teachers pay less attention to girls than boys from the nursery school onwards, that girls are persuaded towards some traditional roles by choice of school subject (they are encouraged to cook but not to do metalwork), that they are persuaded away from traditionally male preserves (science and the technologies), and they are given sex-biased career advice. If they manage to overcome these hurdles they meet, it is said, more or less open prejudice: they are not admitted to training courses of a traditionally male kind even if equally or better qualified, they are regarded as 'odd' if they succeed in 'a man's world', and they are passed over in promotion or given less favourable conditions of service. So education for girls tends to be less effective than for boys for purely sexist reasons. Nevertheless, without any complacency, it has to be said that things are changing and the pace of change will inevitably accelerate. Obviously the issue of genuine equality is one which must be grasped by every teacher.

Similarly, there has been a series of ugly scenes in the education world over racial issues. Even the latest Government report, the Swann Report, on educational opportunity for minority groups failed conspicuously to produce a unanimous statement of the problems and how to tackle them. In 1986 Ray Honeyford, the headmaster of a Bradford school where 80% of the pupils were from ethnic minority groups, was forced to resign after a series of controversial statements in journal articles and there were ugly scenes outside his school each day with small children being actively encouraged to shout abuse at him. Some time ago in America extensive IQ testing purported to show that blacks were of inferior intellectual calibre compared with whites and some other minority groups. A vitriolic debate ensued about whether this was due to inadequate testing methods, language or culture bias in the tests themselves, inherent lack of intelligence in blacks, or other factors. In Britain the psychologist Hans Eysenck fuelled the debate by favouring the theory of lower inherent ability among blacks. The issues here cluster around such questions as how teachers can best understand and use the children's own culture; how differences of personality, language and experience characteristic of minority groups can best be harnessed in British school contexts; and how a more community-based approach can assist teachers to better understand and meet the needs of these young people. The issue of prejudice has to be addressed: and nowhere more so than in the relations between black people and the police and in the employment prospects of black youths, which are vastly worse than those of white youngsters. The role of black teachers must be defined; there will undoubtedly be more of them; and the whole question of boundaries

114

between cultures (how far the ethnic and the British cultures should merge, how far remain separate in the individual's experience) must be addressed. This decade has seen some terrible examples of racial conflict on the streets of major English cities, and it may be that teachers will play an increasing role in providing a climate where tolerance will replace antipathy on all sides.

Any chapter on issues and values in education could go on *ad infinitum* to list and discuss matters of concern. To end this chapter I think it appropriate to shift the perspective from pupils to teachers. One very significant contemporary issue for teachers themselves is one of accountability. In the midst of current negotiations about pay the Government has insisted on the reconsideration of teachers' conditions of service. These conditions of service cover such relatively trivial issues as whether teachers should or should not be paid for lunchtime supervision. Much more important is the wish of Government, and of employers too, to find means by which a teacher's performance can be measured. The matter has been building up for many years, often because of anomalies in the system. So, for example, a probationer teacher newly appointed to a comprehensive school is likely to be teaching thirty-three lessons out of a possible forty in the school week. The teacher's head of department – presumably a much more experienced practitioner with a more complete range of skills to offer children, quicker at preparing lessons and with a fund of materials on which to draw – may be teaching for twenty-five to thirty lessons a week. A deputy head, possibly promoted as much for teaching skill as for administrative ability, may see a classroom for only eighteen lessons per week. The promotion structure thus may appear to favour promotion *away* from classroom contact by the very people who are best at it. Similarly a young Lecturer I in a College of Further Education will be teaching for perhaps 21 hours a week, while an experienced Principal Lecturer may have only 13 hours of contact time. Conversely, while criteria of excellence at teaching itself may be hard to establish and may as yet not be adequately rewarded, so criteria of incompetence must be articulated so that inadequate teachers are not allowed to stay in post to the detriment of generations of pupils.

Teachers should be accountable for their pedagogical skills. Since they are employees, and public employees at that, a number of people or groups have some moral right to expect accountability: the Department of Education and Science, the LEA, the headteacher, parents, school governors, pupils. Over the next few years it is fairly safe to predict that this issue will have to be faced and the public will have to decide: To whom are teachers directly accountable? On what specific issues are they accountable? How can their performance be measured? What should happen if it falls short? Should outstanding performance be rewarded and, if so, in what ways? How should this accountability relate to the overall structure of the profession?

If you decide to go on to teacher training it is likely that these issues will be decided before you qualify, and that the outcomes will affect your career. You will ponder them often between now and that day. For the moment, however, we shall return to the theme of the book. In the last few chapters we have concentrated on the kinds of knowledge that a teacher has to acquire and the kinds of judgements he or she must make. In the chapters that follow we shall proceed to examine what it feels like to be a teacher, first at primary level, then in the secondary age range, and lastly beyond school education.

7

Teaching Young Children

Imagine you are on a fact-finding mission to look at the nature of Britain's primary schools. What pattern of findings would emerge? What variations might you discover? Let's embark on the enterprise and see what we can unearth.

What strikes the visitor to the primary school most forcibly is its busy-ness. Wander through the doors of any primary from John O'Groats to Land's End and the walls are likely to be splattered with colourful posters and children's work; pottery, Lego models, collections of cigarette cards or miscellaneous memorabilia from World War II will fill all available table space; and as the bell goes for breaktime the air will swell with the babble of excited youngsters and the wafting strains of half-mastered recorders. The freshness and enthusiasm of it all will contrast strongly with the rural tranquility or the traffic-torn urban dishevelment of the world beyond the school railings. It is probably this atmosphere of whole-hearted commitment and open-minded discovery that attracts men and women to teach in primary schools. Indeed, after more than 20 years in the profession teaching at every level, it is the opportunity to teach a group of 8- to 10-year-olds that still fills me with the tingling excitement that I felt the first time I went in front of a class. I always know I'm going to enjoy it.

Primary schools do, of course, vary a great deal. Although the statutory age for school attendance in this country is 5 years this does not mean that there is a uniform school system; in fact, even within a single LEA the precise nature of schools may vary dramatically. Here are some of the variations you may discover:

- all-through primaries (5–11 years)
- infant schools (5–7 years)
- junior schools (7–11 years
- first schools (5–8 years)
- middle schools (8–12 years)
- middle schools (9–14 years)
- infant schools with nursery units

Size also varies from the one-teacher rural primary of a dozen pupils to large units of 500 or more pupils on one site.

In general, this chapter will refer to the 5–11 primary school, though most of the principles apply elsewhere.

Once into the school itself an early port of call might be the staffroom. Immediately it is apparent that most staff are women. Traditionally, male teachers have opted or been channelled into secondary schools. This is partly because promotion through the salary scales is better; though at present it remains true that a disproportionate number of male primary teachers reach headships! Young children do need adults of both sexes around so as to learn how to relate to them effectively, and any trend to increasing male presence at the primary level should be welcomed. It remains true that in many small rural primaries the only man the children ever see is the caretaker.

Exactly how the school is organized depends very largely on a whole variety of factors. How large the school is, what the buildings are like, how many staff it has, where it is located, to what degree the head is an authoritarian or a democrat – all these can contribute to the precise details of management.

From the child's point of view, a large school will probably provide most variety. Thus, where there are several parallel classes in each range, the head and staff may decide to group children randomly or to separate them off by ability into streams. This latter course is less common in primary schools, though it does still happen, and may be adopted for the children nearing the top of the junior section

118

even if not at infant or lower junior levels. Again, the chances are that the primary pupil will be in a mixed class; but here and there around the country single-sex schools still exist. On this issue, at least, most people are agreed: single-sex schools do not reflect the realities of daily living and are to be discouraged.

In small rural schools it will not be possible to divide youngsters into traditional age-band classes, so another solution has to be found. In schools with around fifty to 100 pupils the visitor might discover the groupings infants, lower juniors and upper juniors. In smaller schools still (and from choice, too, in some larger ones) family or vertical grouping operates. This means that each class has a full age range within it: 5–7 in an infant only school, 5–11 in an all-through primary. Obviously, the age and ability grouping of the class will have an effect upon the ways in which the teacher organizes the work. Advocates of the less traditional family grouping methods claim that they enable children from an actual family to remain together, that they promote a deeper understanding between children and a willingness to help each other, and that these groupings more nearly reflect the world beyond school. Those who prefer mixed-ability methods emphasize the negative points about streaming: its inherent inaccuracies, its social divisiveness, and its failure to prepare youngsters to empathize with those more or less able than themselves.

School and classroom organization is also dependent upon the nature of the school building itself. Victorian red-brick schools with brown-tiled interiors are still common in urban areas, and were usually built on the closed-box classroom principle around a central hall where all communal or specialist activities (assemblies, PE, plays and prize-giving) took place. Contrast this with a modern glass-sided building, each classroom having exterior doors, leading on to a patio play area and then into the playground and field. In the 1960s there was a spate of 'open-plan' building, in which classrooms as such became extinct, and large communal areas were divided visually into bays and working spaces but were not closed off into small private rooms. Clearly in each of the three cases the whole underlying philosophy of teaching is different. In the first instance it is assumed that teaching is a teacher-dominated, chalk-and-talk activity. In the second we enter the era of the Plowden Report (see page 27), where classroom work was seen as guided by the teacher but based upon access to immediate experience. Finally the approach shifts from teachers and classes altogether into a team-teaching situation in which children learn by having tasks to do and consulting with teachers as advisors and facilitators; the actual 'work' is carried out through pupils investigating freely among the books and resources available in the school and to which they circulate as the need arises.

The organization of learning in the school will also depend to some extent on its management structures, and the larger the school the more formalized these will need to be. Often, where there are several classes parallel in age, the head will appoint one teacher in each year as year group leader. His or her other job will be to co-ordinate the work of all the colleagues working in that age group, checking that they share common aims and objectives, cover similar material, and engage in joint activities such as educational visits.

Another management system is to appoint some staff as consultants. These are usually subject specialists. They have responsibilities across the whole school for an area of curriculum such as reading, language, mathematics or science. Some schools will have more hierarchical structures, with senior colleagues designated to be deputy head or head of infants. Usually there is a mixture of systems: often lines of communication are not immediately obvious, and the new staff member will have to tread warily to avoid susceptibilities!

While some of the management decisions of the school will come directly from the headteacher, most schools also have regular staff meetings. These may include discussions about curriculum, about relations with parents, about school trips, or about major purchases such as a videorecorder or computer. Such staff meetings usually take place after the pupils have left, and they form part of the teacher's normal professional activities.

The time has come, then, to move the ground of our primary school survey into a classroom. In some schools the shape of the school day (the timetable) will be determined by the head or staff in consultation. In others only the fixed points – breaks or the use of shared facilities like the hall – will be determined by policy. In the latter case it is the teacher who completes each day's timetable, taking care that key skills such as numeracy and literacy are covered on a daily or perhaps weekly basis. If there is any such thing as a typical primary day it may go something like this.

Children's early morning arrival in the classroom is an important social time: they enter and chat informally to each other and to the teacher. The teacher will probably have been in the classroom for half an hour or so already, getting displays organized, marking work, preparing visual aids for the day ahead, collecting together equipment. Perhaps some of the conversation will be about the play the class is preparing to perform to the rest of the school at the Harvest Festival. (Primary schools always have a distinctly seasonal flavour, progressing from Harvest, through Hallowe'en and Christmas, to Easter, after which some other event such as Sports Day may take over). During this settling-down period the teacher completes registration, gives out notices and picks up on any problems – a behaviour problem here or a child with a learning difficulty there. In very little time all these tasks will have been done and the teacher settles the class down to the first systematic work of the day.

Our teacher – we shall call her Sue – believes, like most, that it is a sound practice to get basic skills covered while the children are most fresh to pay attention and their concentration spans are longest, so most days begin with number work. This class is using School Mathematics Project (SMP) workcards. A central bank of cards enables each child to work in order through the scheme at his or her own pace. Children sit with friends in little knots of four, but they work individually. Sue circulates from table to table, checking as she goes for signs of inattention on other tables or deviating to help a child stuck on a particular problem. As she looks over each child's work she is not just looking for right answers, but also to spot consistent errors that give clues to the fact that a child has not mastered the material. A failure in addition may be because Kim writes untidily and does not align her columns properly. Mark, meanwhile, simply hasn't mastered the concept of area and his mechanical approaches to the examples on his card show he doesn't understand *why* the sum is calculated in this way. It is a busy lesson, with children at varying stages of the scheme weighing everyday objects, measuring desk tops and making paper cut-outs to explore triangles. Before the break bell goes all the equipment has to be restored to its proper place in readiness for the next day and the children have to complete a record card showing the stage they have reached in the scheme. They go enthusiastically to break, to buy crisps or a chocolate bar and play football or just catch up on yesterday's gossip.

After break Sue has planned a change of pace. Each child has a class library book and the first job is to take this and read it privately. The books are graded by the teacher for difficulty. Each day she calls on two or three pupils to come up to her desk, to read a short passage aloud, and to recount some part of the story. In this way she can monitor their progress in reading skill and can keep individual records to be handed on next year or discussed with parents on Open Evening. One child has come to the end of his current book and he is following the usual custom in this class of writing a short review of his book, saying what it was about and what he particularly likes and dislikes about the story or the story-telling. Sue is especially aware of the need to develop children's critical faculties and of the cognitive importance of skills such as comparing and contrasting, analysing, reasoning and explaining. Once she has seen the work of three pupils, however, she feels it is time to go on to a less self-directed part of this language lesson.

For the first time today what follows is a fairly traditional 20 minutes of 'chalk-and-talk'. Sue wants to help the pupils become more proficient at seeking and finding information when they are doing topic or project work. The classroom has a good stock of books on the current topic: colour.

There is also a school library. But children have to know how to get the information out of the books. Last week she demonstrated how the books are classified, and how to find a book relevant to the theme. Next week she will tackle note-taking. But today it is how to use the contents page and the index. She has brought several books with her: textbooks, encyclopaedias and so on. She demonstrates how each is laid out, where to find the contents and index, how these are useful in tracking down information. She works through several examples. Then she hands out a worksheet that she prepared at home two evenings ago and ran off on the school copier yesterday. The sheet asks the children to find particular pieces of information using particular books. They carry out the practical task of locating books and finding appropriate sections, pages and entries. This is a good activity just before lunch, when attention might otherwise be a little jaded. As the bell approaches she calls them all together and sends them orderly but still enthusiastic to tackle the meal of their choice in the canteen, reminding them as they go perhaps that yogurts are better for them than doughnuts. It is not Sue's turn for eating in the canteen with the children nor to keep an eye on the playground so she will eat her own sandwich and yogurt in the staffroom and trade news with colleagues about pupils or about arrangements for next week's visit by the Road Safety Officer to check over the children's bicycles. Tomorrow lunch-time, by contrast, she will be teaching the beginners' guitar group and lunch will be a hurried and less social affair so she will make the most of today!

The first session of the afternoon is the longest of the day, and is the one where sustained activity is most appropriate. It is used by Sue for integrated project work on the current topic, colour.

The colour topic is being explored by the children both as a class experience and individually. The approach is interdisciplinary, with insights from science, aesthetics, history, geography and English all intermingled around the theme. When the topic started several weeks ago, Sue conducted a 'lead lesson' afternoon designed to stimulate the pupils' interest. She began with a darkened classroom and played mood music while using the slide projector and coloured cellophane to make the walls glow with an appropriate colour to match the mood. The children later matched their own colours to pieces of music to see how far they agreed with one another and why. Then they went on to explore how colours affect everyday life in traffic lights, in indicating the seasons, in the warning colours of wasps, and the problems of colour blindness. Finally on that first afternoon they discussed colour in poems and listened to examples read by the teacher. Since then each child has selected a colour theme of his or her own to explore and write up in a topic folder; so today this is the activity in progress. We can overlook one or two pupils' work to see how they are getting on.

Sophie was interested in the traffic light example and has gone on to look at other signal colours. She has already compiled some information about national flags and the significance of their colours. In the process she found out that, in the Royal Navy, flags are used to convey messages, so she is busy hunting out examples such as quarantine flags.

Mark is a keen insect watcher and, taking his cue from the wasp example, he has set out to see how colour is used in nature. He started with warning signals, and found out that several kinds of moth use bright underwings to flash 'keep off' signals to predators. He's busy constructing a cardboard moth with movable forewings to demonstrate this to the class when they pool ideas at the end of the topic.

Jane is a slow worker, but she has become interested in how colours are mixed so that primary colours make others, and she is fascinated by the many different shades there are of each basic colour. She has been to the local hardware stores and made a vast collection of colour charts and is just on the verge of discovering that each separate shade is given a British Standard number so that it can be reproduced accurately, for example in several different batches of paint.

This work continues with a humming enthusiasm until break, Sue constantly moving to check that pupils are working, to keep an eye on progress, and to make suggestions for new directions.

By the final session of the day every one has worked hard and productively, and there is a real danger that tiredness will tell on the pupils. So now the teacher judges the time is ripe for another change of pace. She brings them out of their seats and settles them close around her in a horseshoe. This is story time. She has found a racy tale of rivalry between the Black Bear and the Red Fox. With actions and changes of voice to fit the characters she holds the youngsters' attention until 5 minutes before school ends. Then it's a quick tidy round, an orderly dismissal, and off they go with a problem to solve overnight to sustain curiosity: Why do you think our 'blackboard' is actually green? There's just time for a rapid cup of tea in the staffroom before our teacher is off to the gym to gather up the netball team for an inter-school match.

During the match, and while she is travelling home, three professional concerns are on Sue's mind, and since we are able to share her thoughts we can examine each of those in turn.

The first and most pressing issue is that it is the practice in this school for every teacher to make a forecast each half-term of work to be covered and to write this up in a Record Book for scrutiny by the head and year group leader. As half-term approaches Sue is thinking more and more about her forecast of work relating to the second part of the autumn term.

The Record Book is a time-consuming affair but it is worthwhile. It is a formalized way of ensuring that each staff member is well prepared. It provides information to other teachers about the progress the class is making, and also to a substitute teacher if our teacher should catch 'flu and go sick for a week. Above all, it fulfils the professional requirement of the teacher to be accountable for her work and its quality directly to the head, and indirectly to the officials of the LEA and to parents. So Sue is mulling over some crucial questions. How and when should she bring the colour project to an end? Has she achieved, and have the pupils achieved, the aims she set out last half-term in the Record Book? What innovative activity can she include to lead up to the Christmas period? What will be her specific aims in the areas of numeracy, reading and literacy for the next 6 or 8 weeks? Is the curriculum she is planning reasonably balanced to ensure a range of subject perspectives? All these and other considerations must soon gel into a series of proposed weekly timetables, schemes of work, and sets of aims and objectives.

Sue's second concern is for next week's meeting of the Parent–Teacher Association (PTA), of which she is a staff representative. Primary schools, even quite large ones, have relatively low capitation allowances – that is, the sum of money per pupil allowed them by the LEA to buy books and equipment and to go on educational visits. Many find that special equipment, a better library collection or more imaginative out-of-school work, can be achieved only through fund-raising. Usually the vehicle for this activity is a PTA or Friends of the School group. As it happens the PTA in Sue's school held a successful summer fete and has amassed a goodly sum to donate. At the forthcoming meeting there is to be a debate as to how best the money might be allocated. Some parents would like to see it put towards a swimming pool, on the grounds that all children ought to be able to swim. The head is known to be opposed to the idea because a pool would attract running costs, and would be usable for part of the year only. He would prefer to embark on a mini-bus project so that children could be taken more easily to local places of interest and go on camping and field-centre visits during the Whit and summer holidays. But Sue knows the same reservations apply to this idea as to the swimming pool. The staff want her to press for the setting up of a spare classroom as a resources room with slides, tapes and video tapes for loan and with viewing facilities for children. She is beginning to formulate her thoughts about how best to present this alternative strategy without alienating both her headteacher and the generous parents who have contributed the cash.

The third issue which is occupying Sue's mind as she

nears home is about her own career. She has three years' experience now and would like to move on to broaden her experience and to gain promotion. She wonders what particular kind of job to look for, and what in-service training she should undertake in the next few months to help achieve her goal. She is torn between two strategies.

Initially she had considered trying to gain a consultant's post, and she would like to do this in the area of science or environmental education. She has seen a Diploma in Primary Science course advertised at the local College of Education to run from the next September and is considering making an application. But her alternative strategy would be to become a year group leader. Her headteacher has recommended this latter course of action, and so she feels that in the short-term perhaps a better option would be to attend the evening course in management to be run by the LEA's advisory service. If she were not immediately successful in obtaining a suitable post afterwards she might consider applying for secondment to the local university's department of education in a year's time, perhaps to read for an MEd with a science or curriculum bias.

For the moment the problems are unresolved, for our teacher has reached home. A meal, some thoughts on the next day's lessons, and it will be time to snatch some sleep before the hectic whirl of the classroom begins again.

Our bird's eye view of the primary classroom has, of course, been very selective. It has served merely to illustrate a not untypical day. Much has, inevitably, been omitted. The description is more applicable to the junior teacher than to the reception infant teacher, for example, since at this latter age the children need a great deal more help with social relationships and with motor activities such as tying shoelaces or buttoning shirts. Nevertheless, the essential flavour of a primary-school day is encapsulated in what has gone before and it remains only to put together some more objective information which amplifies the outline already given.

Obviously in a book such as this one concentration has to be upon the question: What kind of person makes a good primary teacher? The requisite qualities are many, but it is not hard to list the most necessary.

First, the teacher of young children has to have a natural warmth and a good deal of patience. A calm, unruffled adult is a source of great confidence to the young. But this calmness has to be combined with both physical energy and mental agility. The primary teacher has to be both specialist and generalist, and, in the words I used to use to my own primary trainees, 'the first ingredient of successful work in this sector is to be both interesting and interested'. The calm but enthusiastic teacher provides a healthy psychological climate in which learning can take place. This climate is then furthered by firm, but fair and consistent, approaches to discipline and classroom organization. Not only must teachers be impartial, but they must be seen to be so.

The primary teacher, too, will know each child by name and background. Often the teacher will meet the parents informally at the school gate, so a friendly and professional approach is called for. In the classroom the children's initiatives must be valued; and to draw the best out of the youngsters it will be necessary to get down physically to their level for much of the time as well as seeking new and exciting ways to present material.

All teachers need to be organized and to plan ahead. In the primary sector there is maximum emphasis on the pupil as an individual, and so the teacher will have to cope with many different tasks in progress at once. If you are disorganized, forgetful or simply panicky then working with younger pupils is not the task for you!

It has been estimated that effective primary school teachers may, in the course of organizing and monitoring children's work, make several thousand interpersonal contacts each day. That represents a high toll in terms of nervous energy, and so it reinforces the particular strengths that young teachers can bring to this age range.

As we have seen, primary teaching is also most demanding in terms of the activities that go on out of class in the lunch break or after school. It is certainly not a job for someone who is looking for the superficial image of teaching as a

9–3.30, 39-weeks-a-year · passport to a reasonable wage. Those few who do not get deeply involved beyond school hours sell the profession, and above all the children, short.

To end this chapter, mention should be made of findings from the most far-reaching research study into what goes on in primary classrooms in recent years, which is located at the University of Leicester. Known as the Oracle project, this work has resulted in a steady stream of publications. Below are summarized, albeit briefly and superficially, some of the conclusions of this research; and further reference to the book's concerns will be made in the Recommended Reading section at the end of this volume. These findings represent both a view of the current state of play and a blueprint for future professional development.

The study concludes that, contrary to public opinion and some more extreme press reports, the primary curriculum is generally quite traditional and continues to place major emphasis on numeracy and literacy.

Observations made during the Oracle project also exploded the myth of informal classrooms which lacked discipline or teacher control of curriculum. Quite the reverse was true: generally, pupils were purposefully employed in orderly classrooms.

Teachers in the primary classrooms observed did give pupils individual attention and did also individualize tasks for children, as the Plowden Report nearly two decades earlier had recommended.

Plowden also recommended a problem-solving, questioning, discovery approach by children to learning. In general, the Oracle project did not find such approaches widespread.

Class sizes in the primary schools observed averaged thirty pupils – too large, in the opinion of the researchers, for effective use of discovery methods. Such teaching methods in large, mixed-ability classes present acute organizational problems.

Whole-class teaching was practised in the studied schools and, contrary to the Plowden ideal, it was here – not in individualized learning situations – where higher level thinking was demanded of pupils.

Many people think of primary classes as being organized into groups for *learning*. In fact, the Oracle research discovered that such groups are largely illusion: they are for *seating* purposes. Tasks are carried out individually or on a whole-class basis.

For children to engage in effective group work would require certain prerequisites from them: high task involvement, mutual understanding and tolerance, the ability to discuss sensibly, and a questioning approach.

These skills have to be learned, and so such group work needs much preparation before it can become operational. Few teachers currently achieve this.

The Oracle researchers went on to draw out several implications for the future development of primary education:

1 The need to increase problem-solving activity by pupils.
2 The importance of trying to find ways of increasing periods of teacher–pupil contact on a one-to-one basis.
3 The need to avoid using workcards as a teacher substitute, since these lead to boredom.
4 More effective use of monitoring procedures to track the progress of individual pupils.
5 Wider use of team teaching methods and consultants.

With these thoughts in mind you might like now to look back over Sue's day to try to discover how effectively, in Oracle terms, you think she is coping. When you have done this you may care to scrutinize chapter 1 of this book again, measuring the teacher there against the same criteria. In carrying out these activities you will be taking your first steps on the road to the kinds of classroom observation you may be asked to do as a student-teacher, albeit at second hand.

8

Teaching Adolescents

We saw in the last chapter that different areas of the country differ slightly in the ways in which schools are organized. So it is with the secondary sector. Some pupils find themselves in 14-plus third schools, some in selective grammar or secondary modern schools. Some leave school at 16 to enter a sixth-form college. But most now attend large comprehensive units of a thousand or more pupils from 11 to 18 years of age and drawn from a large cluster of neighbouring primary schools. In rural areas these schools serve outlying villages, and over half the youngsters may arrive on school buses each morning. Since these large comprehensives are the most widespread, an imaginary, but typical, school of this kind forms the background to this chapter. Despite variations in organization, size or age range, the principles of teaching adolescents remain fairly constant anyway.

Again it will be helpful if we adopt a 'day-in-the-life' approach to the work of a young teacher in the comprehensive school. What range of experiences is he likely to face?

Since they are so large, comprehensive schools tend to be more hierarchical than primary schools. Management of the school is vested in the headteacher who also takes personal responsibility for boys' welfare and discipline; but in this school there are also three deputy heads. Mrs A shares responsibility for welfare and discipline, especially as they impinge on girl pupils. Mr B runs the timetable, and matters concerned with room allocation and daily administration. Mr C has the duty to overview the school's curriculum, matters such as pupils' performance in public examinations, and the in-service training of staff; it is his job to look after probationer teachers. Generally, teachers who need to take up any of these issues report to the appropriate deputy rather than directly to the headteacher. The school office, situated in the main entrance hall, is well staffed and is the frontline administrative centre for pupils, parents and visitors.

Our teacher belongs to a department. There are ten departments: English; maths; science; humanities; craft, design and technology; home economics; physical education; art; music; and modern language. Some of the departments are very large. Each has a head of department; but some have sub-heads: so science is divided into physics, biology and chemistry, and humanities into history, geography and RE.

Our teacher – we'll call him John – is one of twelve teachers in his department; he is the newest and youngest. Nevertheless, he is pleased with the post because the head of department has given him a good range of classes of all age-groups. This means he has to prepare a lot of very different material, but at least he is getting the flavour of the whole range of teaching.

John teaches English. He knows all the other English staff because he attends regular departmental meetings. Whole-school staff meetings are rare: usually for in-service activities. Communication with staff from the head and deputies is by daily bulletin; staff communicate with each other via pigeon-holes in the Common Room. This Common Room is modern, with a coffee bar that functions at morning and afternoon break and at lunchtime. A majority of staff gravitate there at least once a day, so it is a good meeting place. But in such a large school it is inevitable that the walk from the outlying blocks is too demanding for some! Here and there an isolated department has set up its own unofficial territory in a store room; so there are some colleagues whom John recognizes only distantly.

The day begins with a form period. John is form tutor to 1 Grace. These are first-year pupils of mixed ability: the forms are not differentiated by letters, lest these be construed as denoting pupils' abilities, but by the names of famous cricketers. The purpose of the form period is for the tutor to get to know each pupil individually, and for each pupil to be able to relate immediately and well to a member of staff. In addition to the departmental structure for academic matters, the school has a pastoral system consisting of the Heads of Upper and Lower School, Heads of Year, and form tutors. John usually spends the form tutor period encouraging the youngsters to do homework or borrow books from the class library to read; he tries to circulate and talk informally to individuals. Sometimes he feels there is something they particularly want to talk about – a change of school rule, perhaps – and then he holds an open discussion. When the bell goes for the end of the form period it is off to the English Suite – half a dozen rooms a block away – where there is access to specialist books and resources. Here he will meet his first class of the day: 5G2. Since the nomenclature of the classes is a bit confusing we should digress to look more closely at it.

Pupils entering the school are randomly assigned into mixed-ability groups, each group distinguished by the name of a cricketer as we've seen. At the end of the second year these pupils are then assessed for attainment in their various departments and are re-allocated to three broad ability bands. For teaching purposes each band is sub-divided into classes. At the end of year four final decisions are made about whether pupils will take GCE or CSE public examinations. So pupils progress through the school as shown in table 8.1.

John's session with 5G2, then, is an examination-orientated lesson with those pupils taking a large cluster of GCE subjects only (not CSE), and he is teaching them towards the English Literature paper. They are studying William Golding's *Lord of the Flies*. Last week they had attempted a mock GCE question which asked them to analyse the character of Jack in the story. Today they are receiving back their efforts and discussing with the teacher their omissions and the key points they should have made. These 15- to 16-year-olds are quite sensible, obviously motivated, but old

Table 8.1 *Classes at a typical comprehensive school*

1 Appleyard	2 Appleyard	3 A1	4 A1	5 G1	GCE only	Sixth form for those adding to 'O' levels or seeking 'A' levels
1 Compton	2 Compton	3 A2	4 A2	5 G2		
1 Grace	2 Grace	3 A3	4 A3	5 G3		
1 Hobbs	2 Hobbs	3 A4	4 A4	5 C1	CSE with some GCE	
1 Larwood	2 Larwood	3 B1	4 B1	5 C2		
1 Sheppard	2 Sheppard	3 B2	4 B2	5 C3		
1 Sutcliffe	2 Sutcliffe	3 B3	4 B3	5 C4		
1 Voce	2 Voce	3 C1	4 C1	5 R1	Some CSE	
1 Wardle	2 Wardle	3 C2	4 C2	5 R2		

enough to feel their feet in the school. There are no discipline problems: class and teacher have a good rapport. John feels he is actually aided in this by his comparative youth and inexperience. They share a lot of interests, and usually for a few minutes at the end of lessons, discuss the local disco, the cinema, or the pop charts and the people in them. This conversation is characterized by banter: the youngsters have to explore to find the right balance of informality and respect. John controls the atmosphere by expression and tone as much as by what he says. One or two of the girls can be a bit flirtatious: the boys are quick to notice and he has to make light of it:

'Here, sir, what do you think of Princess Diana? She's not as beautiful as me, is she?'

'You'd better ask your boyfriend about that, Karen; when are you seeing him next?'

John always comes away from 5G2 feeling confident about his abilities both as a teacher of English and as a teacher of adolescents. He feels that, as he gets older, he'll still keep the interest of pupils of this age because they are essentially looking for adults with whom to identify and with whom to share insecurities, however brashly expressed.

The next lesson inspires John with rather less confidence. It's 3C1. This is a group which contains some quite slow learners; but they are also of just the age when adolescents seem to combine apathy towards school with moody antagonism towards all authority. He's asked advice about this, and is only a little comforted to discover his colleagues share his assessment of the situation. The issue of discipline underpins most of the problem and he's had quite a bit of advice. The general opinion seems to be that he must be firm until he is fully established. That means always arriving ahead of the class, controlling the pupils' entry to the room, getting and keeping silence before beginning the lesson and moving round the class so that his presence is felt everywhere. But he feels insecure. Nevertheless, he remembers his college tutor's advice: however nervous you are, never show the signs – ooze confidence, don't hesitate, make decisions and get on quickly.

The youngsters arrive. Generally they don't engage him in conversation as the fifth years do. Instead they are mildly aggressive with one another, verbally or with pushing and shoulder-checks in the queue outside the classroom. He walks up and down the line, fixing eyes on the trouble-makers; things subside and he lets them into the room. One particularly difficult boy he makes sit in the front centre desk despite scowls and mutters of innocence and protest.

Today, John has decided on a new approach. He wants the class to think about writing stories. So he's brought along a short story on tape. This gives him some initiative because he can set up the machine on the front desk, switch it to play, and move to the back of the room. From here he can watch that all the pupils are attentive and not creating any diversion. The pupils listen once to the story to get the flavour; then he gives them paper. They listen again, this time listing three or four things that make the story interesting. The boy on the front row objects:

> 'But it's rubbish, sir.'
> 'If you think so, Steven, write a list of reasons why it *isn't* an interesting story. Later we're going to write our own. You'll have a chance to do better then.'

Steven is momentarily lost for words and for a while tries to spread his disaffection by staring ostentatiously out the window. Today this behaviour fails to interest the other pupils, so John ignores him. He settles, like the others, to the task.

When the story is over and the youngsters have listed their points of interest John explains they're now going to use these as guidelines to help them write their own stories.

> 'Boring,' says Steven.
>
> 'What *don't* you find boring, Steven?' asks John.
>
> 'Fishing,' comes the laconic reply.
>
> 'Right, while others get started I'll come and help you get started on a fishing story. I bet some of the people you go fishing with tell some tall stories.'

Steven is mollified; he enjoys attention. The others are quite interested and get on. When the break bell goes John feels a small sense of achievement and wonders if it will spill over into the next lesson.

Over a snatched cup of coffee John manages to get the ear of his head of department to book the use of some of the department's audiovisual equipment for the following week. Then he compares notes on the day with Sally, a young science graduate. She's had a good double lesson practical with year two, sullied only by a minor medical crisis. One pupil has inhaled too long over some heating chemical and on turning green and nauseous has had to be rushed into the open air. Sally maintains that the problems of safety in laboratories is more of a headache than John's never-ending piles of marking in his less practical subject, but John is unconvinced.

Period 3 is spent with 1 Sheppard. This is a large and lively group of youngsters who have the freshness and energy of the primary school about them. They are trying to explore feelings and emotions through role play. Last week John gave them a story to read, about an old man with failing sight and hearing trying to cross a six-lane road. Now he has split them up into groups, and each group has to make up a short play on a similar theme. John has negotiated a room change so that he can use the Lower School hall. The groups thus have space to plan, rehearse and perform without causing undue disturbance to each other or other classes.

All the groups are very task-orientated, and he spends his time just progressing slowly from one to the other to answer questions or make minor suggestions. He judges when the work is done and intervenes to gather everyone together and decide on the order of performance.

Each group takes its turn. The playlets are very spontaneous and uninhibited. Everyone enjoys the humour of the situations created; but in discussion John picks up the serious nature of the problem, too. The actors who have played the old people are asked how they felt, what thoughts were going through their heads. They confess to confusion, and embarrassment at being laughed at. John inter-twines the various comments to link them up to the phrases from the original story, explaining the old man's helplessness and frustration. The class is more subdued when they leave the lesson; but this will pass quickly as they become absorbed in the next task.

The final lesson of the morning is something of a contrast, for John is timetabled just once a week on a voluntary basis to teach games to the lower school. His role is to assist the specialist PE staff. Half of year 2 goes to games at the same time. Boys and girls are usually separated, then some youngsters will do gymnastics with the specialist staff, while others rotate to various outdoor pursuits either with specialists or with interested non-specialists. Today, John has a group which is assigned to practise the long-jump. His job is to assist with the smooth arrangements for seeing the boys changed and on to the field; then to organize his specific activity. He too has to change into track-suit and trainers, so the whole process is quite rushed. Indeed, the pace of secondary-school life with its regular bells and constant changing of teaching group and rooms, is one of the features of which he is most aware.

These games sessions normally pass without incident. Pupils perform as best they can; he encourages the able ones to achieve and the less able or less motivated to enjoy the activity and fresh air. The period is quite short; and suddenly the equipment has to be returned, showers taken, clothes changed and everyone made ready for lunch in the canteen.

As a young bachelor, John finds lunch a high-spot in the day. The choice of meals is very wide, and although the staff mingle with the children to eat, this is a pleasant enough social occasion. Followed by coffee in the staffroom, and a chance to get one's resources ready for the afternoon, this is a time of day for stock-taking.

Having ascertained the flavour of John's teaching we do not need to follow him any further. We would be better employed to pursue him back to his bedsitter in the evening in order to reflect with him on the professional concerns that are exercising his mind at the moment.

The most pressing daily activity for John is marking. The burden of this is increased by, but not solely due to, his teaching subject. It is further compounded by virtue of his involvement with some senior examination classes. He finds that to break even, he must mark for at least an hour every evening from Monday to Friday, and often again on Saturday. He has evolved a system of getting up early on Saturdays to spend the first half of the day marking, and preparing his lessons for the following week. He can use some of his old college lesson notes; but most lessons have to be prepared afresh, and this is true of the whole of the examination work.

To add to his professional activity he has signed up for a course being run by the secondary adviser one evening per week. The course also involves several residential weekends throughout the year. John feels it is important that he should keep studying the professional side of his teaching role; but it is quite demanding to be both teacher by day and student by night. The theme of the course is Teaching Skills, and he keeps up with it mainly because he is finding it helpful in his daily work.

So far the course has looked at a number of skills which he has found directly applicable to his own classrooms. There have been a number of sessions on question technique. John was amazed to learn that he was destined to ask at least one and a half million of them in his professional career, but the knowledge has made him more determined to do the job properly! So he has discovered that questions can be open or encouraging of pupil responses and speculation (what do you think of Jack's action?); or closed and exclusive of pupil contribution (Jack is the sensible one, isn't he?) The course director has encouraged John and the others to tape-record some of their lessons and then to analyse all the questions into open or closed categories. John has not been too happy with the results, and since that session he has been working hard in lessons on his question technique.

The course has also concentrated on getting John and his colleagues to look at the level of cognitive demand made by their questions. Using the same tape-recordings they have tried to decide what percentage of the questions asked pupils only to revise and recall, for example, and what percentage made the pupils analyse situations or make critical judgements. Since being involved in this session John has tried to prepare his lessons in such a way that in both spoken and written questions he has avoided pupils regurgitating bits out of textbooks. He's been concentrating on developing their thinking skills. After all, his pupils are all in, or entering upon, the stage of formal operations; and their learning should reflect this. He is rather bothered that the examination syllabus, especially at GCE level, does not concentrate adequately on pupils' abilities to think. This means that both to teach effectively and to cover the syllabus he has to work very hard in preparing his lessons in order to have just the right blend of the two activities. Preparation in the early years of teaching is very time-consuming since there is no stock of previous experience on which to build.

The current session of the course is looking at slow learners in mixed-ability classes. He is beginning to pick up some useful techniques. For example, he is no longer trying to set a single task to the whole of his first-year, mixed-ability classes. Sometimes he provides worksheets with a range of questions so that all abilities are catered for; sometimes he divides the class into several groups, each with an appropriate task. In a few instances he is developing 'banks' of tasks so that individual children can be given something more or less specially designed for their individual needs. As part of normal lesson preparation this is extremely time-consuming. John is motivated to pursue this line, however, because he has found that it has helped with the problem of varying concentration span among the pupils. When everyone is more effectively occupied there is more contentment and less likelihood of any disciplinary problem. John considers himself fortunate because his head of department is interested in the skills course and supportive of his experiments with teaching method.

This week's 'homework' for the skills course has been to examine a profile of the qualities required of a good teacher of mixed-ability classes. John has to score himself on each quality, which takes a lot of self-appraisal and some courage. The profile appears below.

A teacher of mixed-ability classes should
. . . prepare lessons thoroughly

. . . not be too dominant

. . . be *au fait* with and value the subject-matter of lessons

. . . ask leading questions

. . . be aware of social groupings within the class

. . . be a good organizer

. . . know how to use feedback from pupils

. . . be able to devise resources and workcards

. . . try new methods of teaching and take risks

. . . admit mistakes and learn from them

. . . know what standards can reasonably be expected from pupils

. . . be able to describe and cope with exceptional pupils

. . . be able to analyse teaching objectives

. . . accept each pupil as an individual

John's other pressing concern is that he is involved in the department's annual drama production. Though the performance is 6 months away, already the staff have started to hold planning meetings after school. The choice of production has been made: *West Side Story*. This means a great deal of co-operation with the musicians, and with the art department, who will supervise the manufacture of scenery and obtaining of props. John is likely to be an assistant stage manager as this is his first involvement; but already the heavy burden of rehearsal is beginning to dawn on him. He wonders what it will be like in September, when he marries his fiancée, and both of them have heavy separate demands made on their time by their respective schools.

Such, then, is a relatively typical day in the life of a young secondary school teacher: and it illustrates well the degree of physical energy, mental agility and professional commitment required.

For our part, we can leave John at this point to look at some objective research carried out into life in secondary schools. In 1979 a major research project known as the Rutter Report[1] gave its views on secondary education. What follows is a summary of its major findings.

The Rutter research looked in depth at twelve inner London comprehensive schools, focussing not on detailed curriculum or teaching methodology but on 'the broader patterns of life in schools and about the kinds of environments for learning which they present to their pupils'. It should be pointed out that all the schools were essentially inner-city in character; they also were in areas where families were highly disadvantaged. The findings are not necessarily true of all schools everywhere. What is instructive about Rutter's work is not the detailed findings so much as the conclusions drawn from them and the conceptual map of schooling which these enable us to begin to sketch in.

The schools differed considerably with respect to the pupils' behaviour and to the attainment of pupils. While it was true that the schools varied in the proportion of their individual intakes which consisted of low achievers, this difference did not wholly explain the variations in behaviour and attainment overall. Furthermore, behaviour and attainment in any given school tended to remain fairly stable and consistent over a period of years. There was also a definite relationship in any given school between, for example, measures of pupil behaviour (regular attendance, truancy, etc.) and measures of attainment (examination successes, pupils staying beyond the statutory leaving age, etc.). In other words, a school which did well on one measure would do well on another; schools which did badly on one tended to do badly on others. Variations between schools did not apparently relate to the size or physical characteristics of the schools, but did appear to depend upon social factors: academic emphasis, teacher behaviours, incentives and rewards, levels of pupil responsibilities.

Rutter concluded that these social factors did not operate singly, but clustered together to form a school ethos. It was this ethos which had a direct causal effect on the behaviour and attainment of pupils. Since schools are social organizations or units, it is not unreasonable, Rutter argued, that they should behave like other social groups – setting their own norms and standards of behaviour, which operate powerfully on the group members.

Rutter then went on to try to isolate some of the elements that go to make up this ethos. They include the following:

1 Good classroom organization by the teacher: preparing lessons in advance, setting up equipment ahead of lessons, arriving on time, gaining attention before speaking, moving quickly and smoothly from one activity to another (transitions).
2 Firm, consistent, but low-key discipline following early awareness of potential problems.
3 The clear expression in the school as a whole of expectations and standards of behaviour and academic work.
4 Behaviour by staff which serves as a model to pupils: for example, showing that they value the equipment or being willing to give up breaktime to discuss a problem.
5 The encouragement of an atmosphere of success in the

classroom and of intrinsic reward or satisfaction in a job well done.

6   The consistency of school norms across all situations and shared by all staff.

7   The acceptance of norms by the pupils, which is probably achieved through providing:
    a) shared activities for staff and pupils
    b) opportunities for pupils to take responsibility
    c) the feeling of corporate success or achievement.
    d) reasonable working conditions for staff and pupils.

8   The even distribution between schools of pupils of low academic achievement, who may be hostile to school and/or the setting up of alternative structures within schools that can provide these pupils too with need satisfaction and rewards.

The Rutter research has, of course, proved controversial. But it does provide real guidance about the nature of schools as perhaps they *should* be, even if its propositions could still be more thoroughly investigated. For the moment you might like to look back over this chapter and ponder the extent to which it appears that Rutter's criteria for effective school ethos appear to be met in John's particular comprehensive school.

9

Teaching Beyond School

The purpose of this chapter is to examine briefly the opportunities for teaching beyond the school level. Included in its scope are the further- and higher-education sector, polytechnics, universities and adult education. It has to be said at the outset that in most cases direct entry to teaching in these sectors is relatively rare, though some institutions offer a limited range of courses for those who wish to enter these levels of teaching. In chapter 12 you will find some details which are accurate at the time of going to press, but inevitably such details are subject to quite frequent change. The chapter itself looks at the variety of routes by which teachers enter the beyond-school sector and tries to reconstruct some of the flavour in teaching students and adults.

When a teenager reaches the statutory school-leaving age of 16 he or she has a variety of choices: to join a YTS course, to attempt to obtain employment, to stay on at school for 1 or more years adding examination qualifications, or to seek a place in a college of further education. Further-education (FE) colleges evolved out of the former technical colleges and have taken over a more distinctly vocational role than schools, even though they may offer quite similar educational opportunities. Nowadays, many of these FE colleges also run higher education courses, that is higher national diplomas or even degrees – particularly in vocational subjects. The work which teachers are called upon to do here is, then, varied both in its nature and its level. Let us look at the structure of a typical FE/HE college, as shown in Table 9.1.

Table 9.1 shows something of the range of subjects offered by an FE/HE institution. Most departments will be offering from half a dozen to twenty courses leading to vocational qualifications from the initial level right through to diploma or degree opportunities. Some colleges are organized by departments, with a Head of Department in charge of each; others use a faculty structure in which there is a faculty head over a range of work with department heads sharing the day-to-day running of specific areas of work. Such an institution would have thousands of students registering annually. Teaching might be full-time; but many courses are offered in the evenings, or on part-time day-release schemes, or as block-release. Unlike a school the student population is ever-shifting; many courses are of short duration only and the building is likely to be busy for 12 hours a day.

Clearly, then, teaching in the FE/HE sector is a quite different experience from teaching in a school – even in a sixth form. Though it is possible to train specifically to teach in FE few teachers come into it by that route. Most will begin by qualifying for a particular job and then progressing in experience to that particular post. Later, such a person may be attracted by teaching his or her subject and so seek an FE post. The chances are such a person will be appointed on the basis of knowledge and practical experience without any training. Once in the system, however, he or she will be encouraged to undertake professional activity and qualification related to the new role as lecturer. So, a trained nurse who wished to teach on the pre-nursing course in the Social and Community Studies Department might be appointed on the basis of her SRN qualification and her nursing experience perhaps with hospital trainees. Once in the post, however, she may be seconded part time to undertake a Certificate in Education course so as more fully to equip her for the role of teacher. This course would be akin to those described in chapter 10.

It should also be said that the City and Guilds of London Institute does offer a FE Teachers' Certificate (CG 730), and aspirants to posts in FE do often take this as a preliminary to

Table 9.1 *Structure of a typical FE/HE institution*

Department	Subjects taught	Faculty group
Construction	Bricklaying; decorating; woodwork; upholstery	
Electrical	Domestic installations; radio/TV repair; electronics; professional qualifications in electrics/electronics	
Mechanical/Production Engineering	Car mechanics; computer-aided engineering; basic metal work; welding; quality control	Technology
Mining Engineering	Specific qualification courses for all levels of the mining industry	
Art and Design	Painting; drawing; ceramics; jewellery; textiles; design techniques and advertising graphics	
Photography	Camera work and processing; specialist and generalist qualifications – e.g. professional qualifying examination – medical illustration	
Humanities/General Studies	English, music, history, geography, etc., plus a range of courses for employment and leisure courses.	Liberal Arts
Social and Community Studies	Pre-nurse training; social work qualifications: sociology and psychology	
Business Studies	Running a business; shorthand; typing; office practice; law	Commerce

Table 9.1 *continued*

Department	Subjects taught	Faculty group
Management Studies	Industrial management; personnel management; trade union studies	
Mathematics	Pure and applied mathematics	
Science	Physics, chemistry, biology	Science and maths
Computing	Programming; computer familiarization; computer applications	

employment in this field. The course does not have the full status of a Certificate in Education, however. The Government is currently exploring the possibility of requiring FE teachers to be trained, and Her Majesty's Inspectorate has recently carried out a survey of qualifications of teachers in FE, no doubt with a view to providing statistics for the Government in this respect.

Teachers in FE/HE institutions are governed by rather different rules and conditions of service from those in schools. They have to be prepared to teach across three sessions, not two, that is during evenings as well as mornings and afternoons. At present lecturers (the usual term) in this sector work a 30-hour week for 39 weeks per year. But there are specific rules governing class contact, so that only part of the 30 hours each week is face-to-face contact with students. Lecturers are graded in seniority, and their class contact hours are determined according to grade:

Lecturer I	20–22 hours
Lecturer II	17–20 hours
Senior Lecturer	15–18 hours
Principal Lecturer	13–16 hours

The nature of the lecturer's role in FE/HE is so varied that it is hard to present an overall picture that would hold true for a lecturer taking, say, 'O'-level-geography groups to one dealing with students for a Mine Manager's Certificate. It remains generally true, however, that most work apart from that which is directly parallel with school work is very practical and highly vocationally orientated. Although much academic study is required of students, the emphasis of courses and of teaching methods is directed much more at employment experience. Indeed, many of the students who come to FE/HE colleges are already employed and are released for a period of time each week. They and the teachers can therefore draw directly upon work experience.

Work in FE colleges is increasingly concerned with teaching youngsters who have left school but are not yet in employment. There are a number of developing initiatives which are being established to bridge the school–employment gap: Technical and Vocational Education Initiative (TVEI), the Certificate in Pre-Vocational Education (CPVE), and the Youth Training Scheme (YTS). There is also a good deal of work in progress with adults who have specific needs: the unemployed, those who need up-dating or re-training, and those who have returned to work or study after a lapse of time.

An FE/HE teacher needs to be flexible in the level at which he/she can work, and sympathetic in approach to a wide variety of older audiences. Also, good experience in a job is significant, as is a practical approach to teaching method. Provided a lecturer can teach high-level courses as well as low-level ones the financial rewards are potentially good, as are promotion prospects for those who are good administrators or managers as well as teachers and academics.

Adult-education courses are sometimes run by FE institutions, sometimes by university extra-mural departments, sometimes by LEAs using school premises in the evening, and even by private bodies such as the Workers' Educational Association. Few, if any, teachers train directly for adult education; and many adult-education lecturers begin life as teachers in schools. They then take local opportunities to teach on one or two evenings per week at their own or a neighbouring school. Some adult-education classes are vocational but many could be broadly described as serving the ends of leisure and pleasure.

Teachers in adult education need to be able to adopt suitable teaching methods for their rather older audiences, a democratic approach in which the learner is very much the decision-maker in his or her own progress (you might like to refer back to the reference to Carl Rogers in chapter 3 on this issue).

Conditions of service in adult education vary according to the nature of the employment and the employer. In practice, financial return often amounts to payment by the hour for a specific class. Part-time involvement in evening adult education by school teachers is an effective way of gaining wider experience and broadening perspectives, but it is also quite taxing as an addition to an already full day's work.

Teaching in a college of education, where students are in training to become BEd graduates specializing in the infant, junior or secondary sectors of education, is something which demands prior experience as a teacher oneself. For this reason, college lecturing is strictly outside the scope of this chapter. But it is a goal to which many teachers aspire in the longer term, so a brief mention is in order.

Most college of education lecturers nowadays probably gravitate towards this work because they have themselves trained to a very high academic level, have had successful and varied teaching experience, and have become specially interested in the processes and methods of teaching (peda-gogy is a shorthand term for this). After a period of 5–10 years in school-level teaching an aspiration to explore the pedagogical aspects of the profession is quite reasonable, and many teachers study for an MEd degree or its equivalent in the techniques of curriculum development or in the methods of teaching a particular subject, age range, or type of pupil such as those with special needs. Such a teacher would be a candidate for a college of education post. Experienced teachers at head of department or headteacher level might also be attracted into college work at more senior levels.

Teaching here is to degree level, and conditions of service

are quite similar to those in FE/HE. There are promotion prospects to senior lecturer, principal lecturer and head of department levels as well as beyond.

College of education lecturers need to be both good academics and good practitioners. The Government is currently concerned to help them sustain continuing classroom experience: a move I would certainly have valued myself during my two spells in colleges. Obviously, these lecturers must enjoy working with students in the 18- to 22-year-old range. A typical week will include a good variety of activities: teaching pedagogy or a subject area, visiting students on teaching practice, conducting in-service training for practising teachers and probably studying for advanced qualifications. It is this variety which makes the role especially rewarding to the individual.

By contrast, it is possible though not common, for people to join the teaching staffs of universities without teaching experience or professional experience in the world of work. Of course, those who teach in the education department of a university will have background and experience identical to those who lecture in colleges of education. Generally, too, teachers in faculties like architecture and law would be drawn from practising and successful professionals. In medicine it would be universally true. But other openings are available, especially in the traditional academic subjects like history, languages or social sciences.

There is no requirement for a university lecturer to be a trained teacher. The more enlightened universities have recently made appointments of staff trainers, whose job it is to help new lecturers especially learn the craft of lecturing and exploit such modern methods as the use of audiovisual aids.

If a university lecturer has not already undertaken research (some are appointed on the strength of a first-class honours degree alone), then the pressure to pursue personal research will be strong. Except in education departments, university lecturers have relatively light teaching loads and short terms. They have quite varied jobs. A typical week might include lectures, a seminar with a small group and tutorials with individual students, supervision of master's or doctoral students' research, and in some cases, laboratory work or visiting students on work experience or teaching practice. There are often quite good opportunities to lecture abroad or receive foreign academics as guests. Highly regarded lecturers may be invited to act as consultants in their field, perhaps to a large company or to a Government department. But always the pressure will be on to research and to publish the results, and this can be a time-consuming task as well as an absorbing one.

Conditions of service for university lecturers are not particularly good. Promotion is from lecturer to senior lecturer, with quite small opportunities to go beyond to reader or professor. Salary rewards at the lower levels are often not commensurate with the high degree of skill and qualifications required.

The university teacher must be, above all, a good academic, highly motivated to read books and journals in order to keep up-to-date with his subject, and dedicated to research and writing. Again, the enjoyment of teaching young adult students is essential as is the realization that many of one's own students will be at least as bright and possibly brighter than oneself – so humility helps!

Finally, in this brief review of teaching beyond school we must deal with the polytechnics. In the 1960s and 1970s the polytechnics attracted a good deal of funding because they were often seen as providing both the degree-level education of the university and the work orientation of the FE/HE institution. In practice, the polytechnic is a mixture of the university and FE/HE. Conditions of service for staff resemble the latter; job specification is quite similar to that of the university lecturer. Since, as with universities, few teachers are likely to *begin* a career in a polytechnic this need not, therefore, detain us further at this stage.

10

Training for Teaching: College and Probation

The three chapters which have preceeded this one have looked at the nature of the teacher's role in different age-range contexts. In this chapter we are now going to explore the nature of training for teaching – that is, to look at what it is like to follow such a training course. Details about how and where to apply for a training course are given in chapter 12. For the moment we will assume that you have made a successful application and are embarked upon the first steps to your chosen career.

At the moment of application you will have opted for one of the two major routes into the profession. The first of these is to obtain a university place in the normal way (see chapter 12) in order to read for a 3-year BA/BSc degree. After the degree you will be intending to transfer from your chosen subject or faculty into the department of education to undertake professional training in 1 year and the award of the Postgraduate Certificate in Education which will qualify you to teach in schools at your selected age range.

For the moment I shall assume that you have chosen the second route, which is to study for the BEd degree at a college of education or in the education department of a polytechnic.

The purpose of the BEd degree is to provide a single professionally orientated course for qualification combining both the subject studies of the BA/BSc course and the practical and educational theory work inherent in the PGCE. It would be fair to say that, as a broad generalization, more emphasis is placed in the BEd course upon education, professional studies and practical teaching than is the case in the degree plus PGCE route.

The pattern of the BEd degree varies widely from institution to institution; but the following pattern, shown in table 10.1, is not untypical.

Table 10.1 *Pattern of typical BEd degree course*

	Subject studies		Education/ professional studies	Teaching practice
	Primary option	Secondary option		
Year 1	Studies in basic subjects: numeracy, literacy, reading, plus a *main* subject	Subject studies: main course and subsidiary course	Courses in education either on a disciplinary basis (i.e. psychology, sociology, etc.) or integrated around themes	One month in summer term
Year 2	Basic subject studies continue, as does main subject; also opportunities for options,			One month in autumn term
Year 3	e.g. in music, art or creative studies, etc.		Perhaps some opportunity to specialize in year 3	Whole of spring term leading to final assessment on teaching practice at end of year 3
	Assessments at end of year 3			
Year 4	Subject studies largely replaced by education elements designed to support dissertation, e.g. research methods, tuition, etc.		Dissertation based on small-scale research for Hons element of degree	Perhaps some visits to schools for short periods to retain classroom contacts

Having established the basic pattern of a BEd degree course let us follow your progress through it. In September you arrive at the college of your choice a few days before the second-, third- and fourth-year students. Some of the staff and some of the older students have come back early from vacation to provide an Introductory Programme for you so that you can get to know your way around. Perhaps you haven't been on an extended stay away from home before, and now, for 4 years, you will be entirely responsible for running your own life as a student. You may be living on site in a college hostel, or in nearby lodgings. You may be sharing a room, and if not you will almost certainty be sharing facilities like kitchens and showers. These early days will help you to get to know the fellow-students in your year-group, so you must make the most of joining in activities. There may be a guided tour of the town, a formal introduction from the Principal, some sample lectures to attend, and some tasks to do. Some of these events will be designed to test your initiative, so you might be briefed and sent out on a survey in the local high street exploring parental attitudes to education. You may have to present a summary of your findings to your group when you get back.

In the evenings during this introductory session there are social events, perhaps a more formal wine and cheese evening with staff. Later there will be student-led activities such as a disco or folk night. The old hands will explain about the Students' Union facilities and answer your queries.

The following week, all the other students return and the buildings will seem bustling and noisy by contrast with the introductory days. Your first few days of official term may well involve visits to local schools to get the feel of teaching; and talks by local teachers and heads. Then the normal timetable of lectures and tutorials begins and will continue for the rest of the academic year.

The chances are that you will find this period an anticlimax. After all the excitement and direct school involvement you have a long period of academic work ahead. There are books to read, essays to write. You go regularly to lectures. There are individual tutorials to attend, when you discuss your own work and progress with a tutor. At first you may find this difficult. In fact, though, you soon discover that relations with staff are quite different from those you had in school. Generally, staff–student relations in colleges of education are friendly and informal: some tutors prefer to be on christian-name terms, for example. Many colleges have a system of 'personal tutors' which means that a tutor is responsible for the well being of a number of individual students. To pursue this role effectively he or she may meet the students informally, perhaps in the bar or at home, from time to time. The friendly atmosphere of the college is dependent upon the fact that you are being trained by professionals to be a professional; and you will be expected to monitor your own levels of work and performance despite this informality.

By the summer term you will be more than ready to get to grips with teaching itself. Of course, you will have some idea of the implications. You will have watched fellow students during teaching practice time. You will know that it takes over the whole of life: writing lesson notes daily, preparing visual aids for the next day, getting up extra early to be at school at 8.30 am, leaving and returning loaded with half a hundredweight of books and materials every day! Conversation becomes decidedly one-track, too!

But at last, after a period of preparatory visits to your school, of lesson planning and monitoring by the tutors involved, it will be your turn to be blooded!

The butterflies always flutter on the first morning. Will you survive your first day? Most people do! Often they observe and teach small groups at first. Then comes the moment when the whole class is yours for 45 minutes. And the time flies past, and you've made it!

Of course, there will have been errors. You may have muddled the order of an explanation or failed to see the minor hair-pulling incident in the back corner. But the teacher and, from time to time, your tutor will sit in on your lessons and help you to iron out your problems. They'll teach you how to look in several directions at once, how to organize the class so you don't have to turn your back on them, how to present your material in exciting ways. You will need, quite rapidly, to get over any shyness at being observed at work because the benefits of allowing yourself to be scrutinized and of listening to the professional wisdom of others are crucial to your development.

Some students find teaching practice difficult and decide teaching is not for them. Most enjoy it. Sometimes it is complicated because the practice school is a long way from college – maybe in a rural area. The college may provide a bus to carry a number of students to outlying districts, or you may have quite a long journey on public transport. A few students are even assigned lodgings near the school for the duration of the practice, returning to college at weekends. Whichever your particular assignment, it is part of your training to cope with its inconveniences. After all, the world of work is not a bed of roses!

Let us deviate at this point to study this teaching practice in a bit more detail. One former student of mine kept a diary in addition to all the other chores. I have included some extracts here to show how one person at least reacted. Notice as you read the extracts how she gains in confidence over time.

Wednesday 5 January
  1 Arrived at school bag of nerves.
  2 Found entrance and went into the staffroom.
  3 10 students together all huddled in the corner of the staffroom forming an impenetrable little clique.
  4 Sat there getting more and more nervous while the staff all hustled and bustled about.
  5 8.50 am bell went and the staffroom cleared. Must be registration.
  6 Sat there waiting – wondering when someone would eventually come and rescue us.
  7 Eventually a couple of us were rescued and taken away, then there were 8.
  8 9.15 am. Then there were 6.
  9 It was then that I decided that if Mohammed won't come to the mountain, the mountain must go to Mohammed. So I made

my way to the first lesson I would be observing – 2W with Melissa Hum.

[*Later same day*]

I walked over with Mr Vision but once we reached the staffroom I was left to myself – the group of students attracted me like a magnet. I sat there through break, my first free period, lunch, my second free period; and Peter Vision said he'd have a word with me about the classes I was going to be teaching. He had a brief word with me, none of which seemed to sink in. The rest of that period was free, followed by afternoon break. Then, last period in the afternoon 4A; one of the classes I had already observed and not liked the look of when I came on my day visit. I sat at the back and observed for the entire lesson, I felt too frightened to even go and speak to the kids and Mr Vision had made no effort to introduce me. I sat on top of the radiator and tried to pick out the isolates, mutual pairs, etc., in the group.

When 4.00 pm came I was quite relieved the day seemed to have passed very quickly despite certain periods of inactivity. Everything was new, there was so much to take in, it was very tiring!

Friday 7 January
I can see the beginnings of the regimental day already – 8.15 am leave the house, 8.40 am arrive at school, take off coat, sit and chat for 5 minutes, go to house and tutor set, etc. . . . It's funny how soon you start to feel 'at home', I suppose it's the familiarity with it that causes this feeling. Tutor set is always a bit hectic, the children can't be quietened for anything more than 30 seconds; despite that they seem a very pleasant group. I feel a bit useless during this time since I have nothing to do, I don't like to suggest that I take the register since it's only Hilary D's second term as a tutor.

Friday 14 January
In fact I was quite glad of the snow because I had the more troublesome parts of 2W missing. Their absence meant I had a much smaller class and, as a result, I would spend more time with each child. The lesson went very well, probably due to the variety of experiments that were available. Mind you, I wasn't sorry to reach the end of the lesson since they'd demolished a beaker, a flask, and a thermometer.

Straight across to 3CPR, no time to collect my thoughts before I teach them. Luckily they are a fairly responsive class and I shouldn't **have** any difficulties. The lesson started well and made

157

good progress although\it didn't go as well as I'd hoped (i.e. as well as it would with Roger teaching). I suppose I'm hoping to be perfect from the beginning, which is very unlikely!

Eventually it was time to go home. I felt full of life until I sat down when all the exertions of the week seemed to hit me. Could I sleep for the entire weekend?

Thursday 20 January
After lunch 7S and their science lesson, they were doing the dreaded topic – human reproduction. I didn't really want to go in because I was sure I would get really embarrassed. However, I went and was really surprised by the fact that I didn't get embarrassed. I think the kids' very matter-of-fact (approaching a 'we know it all, so what can you teach us') attitude helped. I really enjoyed the lesson and felt I was definitely useful to have around, since I was a biologist.

Friday 21 January
Friday appears to be my hectic day although I don't teach every lesson, I'm occupied throughout the day. Next is 3CPR for the same lesson (approx.) that 3P had yesterday. Today they seemed very excitable, why? I've no idea but it was very difficult to keep them quiet so they could hear what they were meant to be doing. Eventually they managed to be quiet long enough for me to explain the experiments to them; immediately I had finished they started work. Their productivity is considerably greater (on the whole) than in the other two 3rd year groups that I teach, many of them had written up most of the work by the end of the lesson; of course there's always someone who does next to nothing! I told them that owing to their misdemeanours last week I had acquired a gerbil – they seemed to think I was cross because of this and loads of them offered to take it off my hands.

31 January
Arm-wrestling
Friday afternoon's English lesson and as usual Mr Ames is late in arriving. Since I have no authority with this class it was a bit riotous. Rather than sitting on the side bench and observing, as I did for the first couple of lessons, I decided to go and talk to the kids. I went over to a couple of lads and asked a few innocuous questions. Once the kids realized I wasn't stopping any activities going on I was called over to a group of lads. 'Read this, Miss' one of them said. Expecting some kind of trickery I read it over to myself but didn't see anything in it, so I read it out – 'the cat sat on

the mat'. 'No, Miss read it properly'. So, I looked again, it read 'the cat sat on the the the mat' but I hadn't noticed. They tried again but I was wise to their little game and it didn't work. Once the kids had seen me fooled they wanted a go. It was amazing how many of them were still reading it incorrectly even although they knew the secret. Some of the lads were engaged in an arm wrestling contest. Michael (who's in my Biology group) said I ought to have a go. I refused. 'Oh, go on Miss' several kids said. I eventually agreed and had a go with one lad – I beat him but it wasn't easy. 'Have a go with Alan, Miss. He's the champion, no-one can beat him'. Foolishly, I agreed and got beaten. They all expected it anyway so we had a good laugh about Alan nearly breaking my arm. At this point Mr Ames walked through the door. 'Miss has been arm-wrestling, Sir' someone said. 'Oh has she indeed' said Dick before telling them all to sit down and be quiet.

The reason I have written this is because I have just read an extract from a journal kept by a teacher in her probationary year which touched on a similar experience (*The First Year of Teaching*, Hannam, Smyth and Stevenson)[1]. She says 'Foolishly, I agree' and then on reflection she's not sure exactly how foolish she was.

Wednesday 9 February
Next lesson is making fire extinguishers with 1S, I've been looking forward to this myself. The intro was very difficult because the kids were so excited but I managed. I also seemed to give the desired impression that it was a dangerous expt because some of the kids expressed some doubts about handling the extinguisher. The kids made up the extinguishers very rapidly and we all went outside to try them out. They worked very well putting out the fire in the waste paper bin rapidly. Once inside the kids wanted to repeat the expt, so we had another lot let off into the sinks. Despite all my warnings about this being a dangerous expt one girl managed to cut her hand when pushing the glass tubing into the bottle.

Monday 7 March
This morning made quite a change from normal since instead of going to school I was going to the university and the abattoir. I wanted some locusts and blood for teaching purposes so I had to fetch them. John kindly consented to be my chauffeur. The visit to the uni was uneventful because I didn't have to pick up the locusts, otherwise it would have been! Next stop was very interesting, if a bit gory, the abattoir is spotlessly clean but the sights weren't –

pigs chopped longitudinally in half, calves' heads with tongues protruding (minus lower jaw), bulls' heads with glassy eyeballs staring out at you and worst of all hot steaming carcasses fresh from slaughter. Despite all the distractions I managed to collect my blood and heart/lung preparations (cost 40p). Getting to school was no problem but actually getting in was because of all the stuff I had, with both John and myself carrying stuff we *just* managed in one journey (I also had rainwater and canal water for my lesson with 2W).

Friday 11 March
Woke up feeling back to my normal self – just as well! Everything went well, got to school on time, tutor set OK, etc.

First lesson with 2W enough to make anybody feel depressed but not me this morning. The kids wanted to carry on looking at water samples for the little things that they could find. Although I'd planned something different I decided to let them examine pond water. The result was it was a good lesson, everything went well and most of them managed to write something in their books! I enjoyed the lesson too, looking at a pregnant Daphnia giving birth and various other peculiar creatures. When I'm very enthusiastic about something it appears to have a very beneficial effect on the kids.

So, like the girl in the diary, you find, quite suddenly, that you have come through a whole year of both practical and theoretical\training and can now rate yourself an old hand.

Your second year in college may be much like the first. The chances are that teaching practice will come round much sooner; and you may well experience the weeks before Christmas in a school. If you are training for the infant or junior sectors you will now discover the levels of excitement which can be generated in primary schools. Academic work will be much as in year 1, but more demanding. Tutors will be expecting you to work more quickly, at a deeper level, and to show more and more evidence of reading. You will have discovered that vacations are designed not so much for rest as to allow you opportunities to reflect on your work and to read all the texts you never quite get around to in term-time. Those who do well academically tend to be the students who read widely, who make systematic notes about what they read, and who revise them regularly.

Your academic assessment is likely to be based upon two separate activities. First, throughout the course you will be writing assignment essays. These will be graded, and so your final performance will be based on the continuous assessment provided by these assignments. Incidentally, you will have discovered that punctuality in handing in work is required and will have developed disciplined study habits to cope with this.

The second mode of assessment is likely to be a final examination in year 3. It is to boost your ability to cope with this that consistent reading and revision are important.

Often the second year of the BEd is the one in which you complete the really significant work in your main or subsidiary subjects: it is a key year in the academic aspect of the course. As it draws to a close you will be aware that quite early in year 3 you will have set your sights on your final teaching practice, which will determine the kind of reference you get when you seek your first post. Indeed, if you do not pass the final practice you cannot be awarded the degree, so you may begin to feel under some pressure. The education and professional studies you will be undertaking in years 1–3 of the course cover ground similar to that in chapters 1–6 of this book, but in more depth.

Once into year 3 the teaching practice and preparations for it take up most of your time and absorb most of your energies. You will be occupied in this for a complete term, and it will be the nearest taste of the nature of the profession you can have until you find a post at the end of year 4 – still some 18 months away! The practice will be watched closely both by the school and your tutors. During tutors' visits you will discuss your progress in detail, this process may also continue in college in the evening. About two-thirds of the way through the practice your tutor will indicate whether you are likely to pass. Some colleges also award a distinction grade to about the top 10% of their students in each year. Potential failure and distinction students, plus a random cross-section of the rest, will be visited by an external examiner. You may be one of the chosen ones!

The external examiner is not there to fail people. His or

her job is merely to be assured that standards are maintained within an institution and also across several institutions. So a visitation should not be construed as being the first step towards the Day of Judgment. Following the examiner's visit all students will be reviewed at a formal staff meeting and a pass list issued. You have passed this hurdle and go on to vacation ready to come back to the final term of year 3 for a reversion to more academic pursuits.

The pace and nature of the fourth year of the Honours BEd is quite markedly different from the work you will have done so far. Usually the major piece of work consists of a lengthy dissertation. This will be an investigation you have carried out yourself into an aspect of education. You will be expected to have direct contact with teachers and children in doing this, and to show that the study has practical classroom value. Early in the fourth year, if not before, you will be trained in relevant research techniques. A tutor will be assigned to you, and you will formulate your research plan. Then from about November to March you will carry out the work in time to write it up for submission perhaps at the beginning of May. Typical subjects might include the following:

1 The 'new geography' and its implementation at St Benedict's Comprehensive School.
2 Remedial pupils in a mixed-ability class: a study of teacher strategies to meet their needs.
3 Case studies of topic work in South Park primary school.
4 Approaches to encouraging creative writing in primary schools: theory and practice.
5 Teachers' attitudes to the new Lampshire syllabus of religious education.
6 A comparison of (specific) reading (or mathematics) schemes in action.
7 A review of the advantages and disadvantages of a problem-solving approach to teaching.
8 The use of the computer in teaching history.
9 Early days in a reception class: a study of the problems

of children, teachers and parents during the first 2 weeks of term.

10 The correlation of musical and mathematical abilities in three primary schools.

In order to carry out this research effectively you will need, with the college's support, to learn about research technique, to decide in detail how to carry out your own study, to plan the various stages of the investigation including the necessary visits to schools, and to carry these through within the available timescale. Your final Easter vacation will almost certainly be spent analysing the data you have collected, ordering it ready for writing up during the early part of the summer term, and reflecting on its significance so that you can write a sensible discussion chapter to end your dissertation. Throughout the whole year, too, you will have been reading all available books and journal articles on your chosen theme to compile the Review of the Literature section of the research report.

In the summer term your work will be written up. You will probably have it professionally typed and bound. Once again it will be scrutinized both in college and by external examiners.

Finally, after four years of hard labour, you will be awarded an Honours BEd degree divided and sub-divided into classes: 1st class, Upper second (2^1), Lower second (2^2), and Third class, and you will be qualified to take up a first teaching post. Now all that remains is for you to secure a suitable post and your professional career will have begun!

The process of applying for teaching jobs is a lengthy one and can be quite harrowing in the current economic climate. You will receive quite detailed and specialist help from your college and the whole issue is beyond the scope of this volume. However, the first year of teaching is a probationary year, which means that during it you are expected to go on learning. Your progress will be monitored by the advisory staff of the LEA in which you work. At the end of it you will be assessed, and only at that point will you be finally qualified as a teacher. For this reason the chapter goes on to look in some detail at the probationary year, since it is part of the training process. Before doing so, however, it is necessary to go back and reflect upon the fact that the BEd was only one of two routes into the profession. So it is opportune to glance briefly at the alternative of BA/BSc plus PGCE.

Those who opt for the conventional university degree as the start of their teacher training should bear in mind two things. First, that the subject studied should have a direct bearing upon school curricula, so aeronautical engineering or classical Chinese are likely to be highly unsuitable degree courses however valuable they are in their own right. Second, a university degree is an end in itself, so you are deferring a career decision by 3 years. Some young people rate this latter course of action an advantage; others do not. The choice is often a personal one.

There is no need to describe a PGCE course in detail since much of it looks like a truncated version of the BEd. PGCE students are not required to do subject studies; but they do undertake studies of the theoretical and practical aspects of teaching. One of the three terms will be wholly absorbed in an extended teaching practice equivalent to the final practice of the BEd course. PGCE students may be involved in continuous assessment, and may take some exam papers. They will attend lectures and write essays just like other students. They will not usually have time to write extended dissertations similar to those commonly found in the fourth year of a BEd Hons course.

An advantage of the 3 plus 1 form of training for some students is that, on completion of the degree, one is free to apply to undertake the PGCE year in a department of education in any other university. Application is made direct to that department, and obviously the departments with the best reputations nationally secure the most promising students. From a student's point of view it gives experience of two universities and of two locations.

The degree plus PGCE route probably requires students to be more subject-oriented, at least in the first 3 years. It is thus often favoured by potential secondary teachers; though more universities are now offering primary-oriented PGCE courses.

This chapter, then, has so far reviewed the routes into teaching, has faced some of the issues surrounding their respective merits, and has tried to examine the feelings and experiences relevant to a teacher in training. For the remainder we shall look at the nature of the probationary year.

Once qualified by the BEd or degree plus PGCE routes to take up a teaching post the new teacher is officially a probationer for 1 academic year. At the end of the year, subject to satisfactory performance, qualification is confirmed and the teacher is issued with a DES reference number.

The nature of the probationary year varies enormously from one LEA to another. Almost the worst are the LEAs which hold a wine-and-cheese evening for all new staff in September and then leave them virtually leaderless until the following July, when the head is asked to submit a progress report. The very worst LEAs are the ones who omit even the wine-and-cheese evening!

By contrast, in good LEAs one or more LEA advisers will have responsibility to visit probationers at regular intervals, to give advice, to put on a number of in-service training evenings or weekends, and finally – in consultation with their head of department and headteacher – to report on them. Most probationers welcome this attention because, however good the training course, the role of full-time teacher will throw up snags which are unforeseen. To illustrate this point we can eavesdrop on three probationers from amongst a sample who were asked to describe their jobs to a research team. They are all in their first year, having come direct from school and teacher training to the profession at the age of 22.

Zena

I teach RE throughout the school. Pupils have a complete blockage about this subject; just the mention of it turns them off. As a result I'm always looking for new ways to approach the syllabus. This involves a great deal of preparation. You can see from the classroom walls that a lot of what I do is visual display work. I find that works with younger children. Drama is a useful medium too.

Take a theme like Christmas. I take eight parallel first-year classes. You can imagine how boring it gets doing the same old story again and again. If I use drama, I can break each class into groups. The groups are given workcards which break the story down into episodes. The emphasis now is on the children: they have to decide how many characters are needed for the scene and how they will interpret the plot.

Organization becomes important here. It's more exciting if the different groups can have space in separate rooms; and they bring their own clothes for dressing up. Preparation looms large, and I'm building up a library of hand-produced workcards.

With older children I use as much film as possible, and videotape. Here the emphasis is on moral issues rather than religion. The lessons are short, only 35 minutes, so work has to be tailored to fit into these small slots. Music is a useful approach: I play the guitar, so for example today I'm going to introduce a biblical theme, with some songs from *Jesus Christ – Superstar*, which are very dramatic.

At present the department consists of three probationers, with the Deputy Head of school acting as Head of Department since there isn't one. Despite this we're trying to revise the school syllabus because neither staff nor pupils are happy with it. We're trying hard to work out a child-centred approach, one in tune with modern thinking about teaching religious education. Some of us would like an integrated approach across subjects; but we're all very inexperienced and it's a tricky issue to handle.

Jim

As a probationer (as opposed to a student in training) I certainly find some things have changed. For example, I don't often get time to write lesson notes. That doesn't mean I don't prepare lessons: the emphasis is more on preparing the actual materials I want. So if I'm teaching about right-angled triangles I have to put together the items I need to demonstrate a 3-4-5 triangle will always contain a right angle.

Class control is important, too, so I go through a series of steps: I arrive early; I control pupils' entry to the classroom; I move to where I can see and be seen by all the pupils; I know individuals; I settle down any potential trouble-makers; I have work on the board ready or equipment prepared; I move around the class to monitor; I don't turn my back on the class; I remember to project my voice; I use names; I move physically in among the children.

In maths, testing takes up a lot of energy. We have a standard series of tests that are administered every year. They have to be marked and the results collated and passed on. I also set my own tests about once a month as feedback to me about how pupils are getting on.

The fourth year are doing CSE which has a modular structure. My job is to cover the ground and to push the slower ones to this end. The modules are marked by me, but it is moderated by an external examiner. I don't have any other direct contact with exam administration.

Substitution duties – teaching in place of absent colleagues – takes up most of my free periods, so over a week almost my whole time can have been made up of class contact.

Paula

I was actually trained as a mathematician: but when I was offered this job I agreed to teach physics and biology to years 1 and 2. So this year, my probation year, I'm teaching biology to year 1; and for year 2 I take physics for a term followed by two terms of biology. It's quite demanding because for the first years I don't have access to a laboratory. We're located in an open-plan classroom, and when we get to the practicals I have to swop rooms by arrangement with another member of staff. The course we use is Nuffield Science; this though is dependent on children working at their own pace. Since I can't provide apparatus every lesson I've had to turn the whole process into a blackboard exercise, and to get the pupils to store up their experiments for the occasional laboratory session. Using a classroom has drawbacks. For example, we had to do some work on fish fins, so all the water had to be carried up to the classroom. When the youngsters do go in a lab it changes their whole approach – much better – and the technicians set everything up ready in the laboratory. Part of the skill of the classroom is to choose work that can be adapted for traditional row seating, which takes a lot of the fun out of it.

We have to obtain most of our own specimens – flowers, worms, etc. There's a lot of forward planning; when we need a fish we go the fishmonger.

I don't have too many problems with slow learners because I base a lot of my work on pictures. The slow learners copy the pictures, while the quicker ones may go on and describe the experiment in their own words or even make deductions. I work out in advance the basic messages I want to put across to everyone in the lesson and the slower ones just do this. For the able children I fall back on the textbook, or on some questions of my own. To keep up the slower workers have to miss out bits of the syllabus that are too advanced. They can keep up the flow of work this way, and it means that when I do chalk-and-talk lessons no-one is lost. On the other hand I'm not stretching the able ones enough.

My second-year classes do have a laboratory, and I've established safety rules. In the same way I have established my own patterns of activity: sandwiches of experimental work and theory. Pupils are very responsive to this now. My only hitch with this group was that we didn't have textbooks at the beginning of the year; but we've put this right.

The head of department and all the staff are very supportive: if I get into difficulties someone will always contribute an idea or suggestion. I've had to do a lot of learning at my own level because I'm not a biologist or a physicist.

Most pastoral problems are picked up by more senior staff; but I may pick up the problem of say, truancy if it occurs among my own class.

The children know this is my first job, of course. This affects their attitude to me and mine to them. Discipline has sometimes been a problem. I think one overcomes this by personality and by anticipating trouble and acting before it happens. Punishment isn't effective, but reporting the child to a senior member of staff is.

I have a system for coping when I start a lesson. First I order the furniture, then move potential trouble-makers away from one other, and get the children to stow bags and baggage away. Usually things proceed satisfactorily from there.

These three quotations give something of the flavour of what it is like to be a probationary teacher but perhaps, too, some other considerations should be borne in mind.

Assuming that the teaching week is divided into forty periods or lessons, an HMI survey found that, on average, heads taught for five, deputies for 18, scale-4 teachers for thirty, but probationers for thirty-three. So the least experienced members of the teaching force certainly carry a very heavy burden: almost the same as scale-1 and -2 teachers. This knowledge must be viewed against the context of teaching as a very stressful occupation – indeed, we have seen already just how many interpersonal contacts there are each day. Many, but not all, will be friction-free. But teachers do tend to 'salivate to the bell' at 40-minute intervals, and to fill breaks with work rather than relaxation.

In surveys of probationers at work, then, it is not surprising to find the following sources of problem occuring most commonly:

● issues about class management or discipline;
● issues about sustaining the correct tone of relationship with pupils;
● issues about teaching in ways or situations for which college had not prepared the student (e.g. a multi-cultural environment or using unfamiliar methods like team-teaching);
● issues about using unfamiliar equipment in unfamiliar locations.

Some individual schools make sure that an experienced head of department, or deputy head keeps an overall eye on the new teacher. A good head tries to ensure that the probationer is not given all the most difficult classes, and has some time in which to see experienced teachers at work. Just as important is the period before the probationer actually takes up the post because it is then that he or she can visit the school, watch pupils at work, get acquainted with the syllabus, read the school handbook, and mull over the detailed specifications of the job.

Teaching is a very challenging profession, and one that demands dedication, physical energy, mental alertness, and highly refined skills as well as a good grasp of the subject matter to be taught. Given effective training and a sound period of probation the new teacher can look forward to a career which is intrinsically rewarding and which offers enough variety to sustain freshness and vitality over many years.

11

Is Teaching for Me?

'Teachers' strike action damages pupils' exam hopes'
'Woman teacher mugged by pupil'
'Schoolmaster elopes with pupil, 16'
'Lords come out against the cane'

These are just a few of the headlines that go to make up much of the public image of the teacher. Unlike doctors (professional, knowledgeable, at the frontiers of research), dentists (white-coated and scary with a whiff of disinfectant), RAF officers (technical wizards performing glamorously at supersonic speed), teachers tend to be regarded in one of two, quite contradictory, ways in the public imagination. They are either humourless, pedantic, and elegantly dowdy in gown and mortar-board, or they are long-haired lefties subverting the impressionable young minds of the next generation of voters. In the popular mythology it goes without saying – though it *is* often said by politicians and others who should know better – that teachers are wholly responsible for the failings of youth, for mugging, violence, indiscipline, the breakdown of family life and the social ills of society in general. But where in all this lies the truth?

This chapter sets out to help you explore whether you feel you are suited to several decades in the profession, but truth about this profession is much less romantic than the fiction, as is often the case in real life! Teachers are a large body of professionally trained men and women of varying ages, background experience, social class, political persuasion and personal ambition. In personality they may range from the introvert to the extrovert; in personal interests and achievement from the Olympic athlete to the antiquarian follower of archaeological digs; in daily life they can be found doing precisely the mundane things every other normal individual does. It is true that teaching demands certain skills and attributes, such as good organizational ability, reasonable levels of intellectual performance, and a certain degree of personal stamina because it is not a sedentary job. What it does not ask, and what it can happily exist without, is professional typecasting.

So do you think you can see yourself in the role of the teacher? It is a role, not a mould. You will not be a stereotype of your own teachers: the world has moved on, children behave differently in each generation, and to fill such a stereotype would be a recipe for failure. But you will have to play many sub-roles within the overall role of being 'teacher'. Here are just some of the sub-roles the teacher may play with respect to one or another audience:

To pupils: disciplinarian, instructor, facilitator, confidante, substitute parent, assessor, hero/heroine.
To other staff: colleague, co-worker, organizer, confidante, friend.
To the head: assistant, delegate.
To the officers of the LEA: employee.
To parents: sympathetic listener, adviser, PTA member.

Let's try to put some flesh on the bones of this sociological insight into the teacher's multi-faceted role. What exactly are you going to have to cope with during your working life? With communicating knowledge, skills and concepts to pupils or students, of course. But obviously it goes far deeper than this. So what circumstances arise in practice for the teacher which make personal and professional demands outside the immediate business of teaching and learning? The headlines at the beginning of this chapter provide just a few clues; but perhaps a logical approach would be to look

171

at the three main sectors of education in turn, beginning with the role of the teacher in the primary school.

The younger the child, the more likely the teacher is to have to act in the role of the substitute parents. This is both a functional activity (tying shoelaces, taking children to the toilet, keeping the classroom clean during the day) and an emotional one, for young children need immediate security and the close physical presence of the teacher. It is important to enter into the psychology of the young child – for example, to sense when he or she is worried – and to anticipate problems by allaying fears with a well-timed story, a role play or by introducing an appropriate toy or providing a distraction. There is a language of small children which teachers tend to adopt, and a tone of voice. In its caricatured form this is often referred to as a Joyce Grenfell approach. Of course, very young children cannot cope with the speed and range of adult language; but it is important as well not to degenerate to the caricature. You will have met teachers who do this; and some who take the same mannerisms and speech into their homes, the supermarket and their own social relationships. Don't imagine that this is necessary or desirable. It is neither!

One specific problem of the young child to have hit the headlines a lot recently is child abuse. Teachers of infant and junior pupils need to be very aware of this. As in everything, however, mature judgment is called for. Many parents do chastise their children physically, and (regardless of whether you as an individual agree with this) society accepts this behaviour as reasonable. So what teachers are looking for is evidence of non-accidental injury inflicted, usually regularly or often, which leaves tell-tale signs: bruised handprints, burn marks, broken limbs that don't correspond to the child's description of the circumstances of the injury. Obviously any normal human being feels outrage at the deliberate physical ill-treatment of a child; but the teacher's role is usually to remain emotionally detached – the teacher reports the incident up the line to the head who will take the necessary action. The teacher, however, must provide unobtrusive classroom support to the child.

172

Another form of child abuse is sexual abuse. Here the circumstances may come to light only slowly through things children say, for there are usually no physical signs as in battering. Incest is much more widespread than is imagined; and victims are often very young. A great deal of sexual abuse takes place not in parks or public places but in the home. Again, the situation has to be handled with tact because it is always essential not to implant ideas and suspicions in young minds when they are wholly irrelevant; and again the teacher at the grassroots level provides the support and help, but the situation itself is handled at a more senior level.

In thinking about the teacher's role in picking up problems that have a domestic origin it is also important to stress that teachers and heads need to avail themselves of as much factual information as possible before jumping to conclusions. I am reminded of a cautionary tale which happened to neighbours of mine. Mr and Mrs Roberts had a child at school. Each day Mark wrote a diary entry for the teacher for the class 'news' board. One day Mrs Roberts was invited for a private interview with the head. She was greeted with great sympathy by the head who probed whether there was anything she could do to help. Mrs Roberts was mystified until she was handed Mark's diary entries. One said: 'My daddy is an alcoholic'. Mr Roberts worked for a shipping company whose major trade was in wine. Unfortunately Mark had made a slight error in his father's job description!

Schools vary a great deal, and the role that you might play as the teacher might alter substantially from one school to another. Living in a village and teaching in a two- or three-teacher school is quite a different experience from life in a 500+ primary school in an inner-city. Both schools may enjoy a rich community life, but the two will be in marked contrast. One may have deep roots in the local soil, the handful of families stretching back over many generations with you as a newcomer even after a decade or two! The other may be rich in cultures from a variety of ethnic origins, with perhaps a rapid turnover of population or acute urban deprivation as a context for your children's homelife. Obviously, then, the experiences you give to children will have to vary according to these particular situations. A day travelling on a siteseeing trip round London using the underground system might be an adventure for children from a rural background; but milking a cow or penetrating deep into a forest might be a more fitting experience for the urban children. At the primary level many children have really very limited experience of the things that educated adults take for granted; devising experiences to broaden children's horizons, awake curiosity and build confidence is part of the teacher's role. This is still education, but it goes beyond a narrow view of classroom learning.

There are plenty of issues, too, about the role of the teacher in the comprehensive school which need to be faced by would-be entrants to the profession. For many, the most pressing is likely to relate to stories or incidents about physical violence from pupils. Are pupils in the comprehensive school likely to assault you? Well, it does happen. It happens for all sorts of reasons. Sometimes a child is out to prove his macho image in a confrontation; sometimes an assault by a boy or girl is an act of frustration at some event beyond the school gates which cannot be tackled directly. Sometimes teachers, because of inept handling of a situation or failure to read danger signals early, provoke or exacerbate violence. But, if you calculate how many man/woman hours are spent in classrooms and extracurricular activities by teachers every year and express the number of incidents of unprovoked assaults on teachers as a percentage of that figure, then you have about as much chance of being attacked in a classroom as you do of dying in a plane crash.

As a teacher of teenagers, however, there is no doubt that you will be face to face on a daily basis with young people's emotional problems. It is, of course, essential that a teacher of teenagers makes good relations with the pupils: so if you are outraged at the latest hairstyle, horrified by teenage culture and wholly unprepared to be moderately knowledgeable about the pop-music charts maybe teaching isn't your scene. On the other hand, it is an error to believe that teenagers want you – the teacher – to look and behave like one of them. What they are looking for is not emulation but acceptance. Firm but friendly classroom relationships are essential; and an ability to be yourself but to relax and communicate easily outside the classroom. Teenagers usually respond to being treated like adults without condescension or ostentation.

It is inevitable, however, that teachers become targets for adulation by pupils. Girl pupils do get crushes on female teachers; teenage boys become sexually aware of women teachers; girl pupils practise sexual advances on men teachers. As usual the key to successful professional behaviour lies in the word balance. The first quality a teacher needs is awareness, to know what is happening. Once aware, the teacher must avoid being tactless. It is not too difficult to avoid awkward one-to-one encounters with pupils, and within the class to pay an individual the same pleasant attention as everyone else – no more, no less. Mild flirtation is used by some teachers as a means of keeping difficult pupils pleasant – what is important is knowing where to draw the line, and drawing it quite firmly at a very early stage.

This question of balance applies to all emotional attachments to children or teenagers that one meets in a professional career. Of course, we all like some children better than others, but professionalism demands we minimize any show of such feeling. Likewise, we all feel sad when a class moves on to a new teacher or when pupils we have known a while leave the school: this is right and proper, since teaching depends on relationships and relationships affect our emotions. But for many teachers, that is where it ends. For a few, they may keep in touch with former pupils over many years; there is no harm in this. Only very occasionally does a school relationship go wrong and result in a scandal, like the 'sex in headmaster's study' headline. Of course, these few incidents attract much publicity, out of proportion to their frequency.

Pastoral problems are frequent for teachers of the teenage pupil. In particular, those concerned with drugs, with sexual

175

relations and with the prospects of employment or unemployment.

As far as drugs are concerned, the issue is quite complicated, The classroom teacher will hardly be involved at all if a pupil takes or sells drugs off the premises and is apprehended. But the teacher should know both what common drugs look like, and also how to read the signs of drug-taking in pupils' behaviour. The wider issues of drug abuse should be dealt with at school level as part of a school policy: the head should ensure that in-service training for staff makes teachers knowledgeable and that there is a policy in the school for education of pupils about drugs and drug abuse. At the classroom level, then, the teacher needs only to be vigilant. If pupils report that they or others have taken drugs the best policy is to consult the appropriate senior member of staff and to allow trained personnel to take over the situation. Drug-dealing is a serious criminal offence; drug-takers are breaking the law, but also need specialist medical and counselling help.

As with drug abuse, so there should be a school policy to ensure when and how sex education occurs in the school. Assuming this is so, what the classroom teacher faces are the personal problems of individual pupils. Pupils, both individually and collectively, do feel the need to discuss sexual behaviour with trusted adults, but do not find this easy with their own parents. Obviously this is an area that many lay people find embarrassing; but an effective teacher will not show embarrassment. It is important to be very honest in answering teenage questions about sex and sexual relations. My own view is that the teacher should not feel the need to advocate a particular viewpoint – e.g. that sex before marriage is/is not wrong. Rather, part of the teenager's learning is to think things out for him or herself; so the teacher's function is to point out facts – the problems associated with sexually transmitted disease, the effect on society of changing patterns of marriage or cohabitation, the range of views about birth control. All these views can be discussed honestly in a conversational way. Some pupils may need individual advice: menstruation causes girls a lot of anxieties, or boys may feel uncertain about handling first dates or a relationship that is developing more quickly than they anticipated. As always, it will be the teacher's own maturity and sensitivity which determines whether pupils do or do not trust that person with their questions or confidences.

One of the hardest tasks for the contemporary teacher of teenagers is to keep up morale and motivation at a time when job prospects are so bleak. It is, of course, no part of the teacher's role to give false hope. Rather he or she has to foster productive attitudes: realism, self-reliance, initiative. These qualities in pupils may help to maximize the chances of pupils to obtain employment while preserving the actuality that, in the end, employment may simply not be available.

The effective teacher will not necessarily take a direct hand in career advice and education in the school curriculum (that is the role of a specific specialist); but at a personal level he or she will know and advise upon further and higher education routes, alternatives such as the YTS, and will help individuals talk through their own aspirations and strategies.

Though this brief review has looked at several common pastoral problems that teenagers experience, there are plenty of others and the good teacher will be a listening ear or will be ready with an open-ended word of advice when approached. It is not necessary to become a trained counsellor or a specialist teacher in pastoral care to do this work; indeed any teacher who falls short in this area is a poor professional. The specialist advisers are best reserved for the detailed or intractable problems; what is needed in most cases is the sensible word of a more experienced and friendly helper, someone who has been through the experience or has a wider knowledge on which to draw.

So far we have looked at the teacher's potential worries about school-level teaching. How does the picture painted here compare and contrast with work as a lecturer in further or higher education?

The first point to make is that tutors in these settings still have to define their roles effectively and to do so in terms of a context which involves the teacher in pastoral as well as academic responsibilities. The FE tutor is still dealing with teenage problems, but often in a slightly more acute form. Unwanted pregnancies, acute money problems for students who have inadequate grants or whose parents do not top up LEA provision adequately, serious relationship problems between teenagers and their parents – these are quite regular issues in which the FE tutor may be involved. How problems are handled may vary between institutions. Sometimes the individual tutor will be quite deeply committed to active help (in the case of a pregnancy, perhaps going to the home and helping the daughter break the news), or he/she may be a sympathetic listener who passes on difficult cases to more specialist counsellors or consultants.

At the HE level students are all over 18 and therefore adult. Tutor–student relations tend to have become more informal. Perhaps students will use the christian names of staff; they may meet socially outside college classes, in the college bar for example; they may develop enduring personal friendships that last a life-time. Whatever the level of education, however, the role of the teacher is always characterized by a level of care, responsibility and confidentiality that transcends the narrowly academic boundaries of his or her role.

Another phenomenon common to teachers of all young people – even at the HE level – is the ability to deal with parents. One still occasionally finds schools with signs outside which are less than welcoming: 'Trespassers will be prosecuted'; 'All visitors must report to the office'. But most schools, and colleges, know the benefits of public relations. 'Welcome' is a more common message than 'keep out' nowadays. There is always the danger that an over-zealous teacher will see the youngsters as 'my pupils' or 'my students'. In fact, of course, parents have heavy responsibilities and wide-ranging concerns for *their* children: we are simply *in loco parentis* for part of each week in term time. Handling parents who are pleased, enquiring or even distraught, is an important skill. For infants' teachers, parents are often present at the school gates or bring children into the classroom., Regular, informal conversation is possible. The teacher is, of course, the professional with a trained eye and a wide knowledge of children's needs. Such a teacher can take initiatives in nipping problems in the bud or in advising parents about warning signs of trouble; he or she can be a consultant for parents; and, above all, the teacher will want to praise the child to the parents when appropriate. The reverse, dealing with school-based behaviour problems by involving parents, should normally be reserved for serious recurrent issues with the knowledge of the headteacher; children's minor misdeeds should not be relayed to parents as this makes the children feel insecure.

At junior and secondary levels parental involvement will tend to be more restricted: invitations to attend assemblies, concerts or plays, or to discuss children's progress at relatively formal parents' evenings. To handle the last effectively it is vital to know all your pupils by name, to have a clear picture of each youngster's performance and ability, and above all to be ready to listen to what parents want to tell you. These may seem elementary preconditions for successful communication; but I was once told by a mother of 14-year-old twins that I was the first teacher she'd known who could genuinely tell her sons apart in both appearance and personality – no great bouquet for me, but a sad indictment of some fellow professionals.

Parents of students at the FE or HE levels are usually involved, if at all, only on formal occasions like graduation. Nevertheless, these occasions may demand some social skills from tutors. In my own college we make a very real attempt to meet parents of 16- to 18-year-old students. Often these meetings occur on occasions when a student develops a problem – perhaps a long-term illness – and it becomes necessary to explain to the parents (in some cases, of course, step-parents or guardians) the implications of the delay in finishing the course. In this way parents are encouraged to continue to be supportive of the student. In the same way, with older students, it is useful if spouses or even boyfriends or girlfriends can feel able to have access to the tutor if difficult circumstances arise.

At the school level, PTAs are common. These are often fund-raising bodies; they may be active within the school, or relatively distant and uninvolved dispensers of largesse. Any teacher may be required to represent the school at such an Association meeting and to meet parents at both the professional and social levels.

So far this chapter has considered the public image of the teacher, some problem situations which might be encountered arising from the teacher's varied roles, some pastoral issues, and relationships with parents. The other set of issues an intending teacher may be concerned about relate rather to the nature of the profession itself. For example, many young teachers worry as to whether, dealing so much with young children, they will lose their ability to communicate with adults and move freely in an adult social community. There are indeed real dangers here; but sound advice is always to make sure that school does not (as it so easily can) absorb every evening of the week with marking, every holiday with a school trip, and every weekend with preparation. Every teacher needs to monitor his or her time to include activities of personal interest, social events, leisure pursuits; and, above all, one's conversation should never become exclusively about school and children – a special danger if you marry a teacher!

Some young teachers fear the boredom of teaching the same thing year after year. In fact syllabuses change rather rapidly; and at a college of education where I once taught, three different BEd syllabuses were introduced in 4 years. My own advice here would be twofold. First, every 2 or three years in your career try to find a new niche: in the current economic climate this may be a partially new role in your existing school rather than a wholesale promotion elsewhere. Second, as a young teacher myself I often had to teach the same chunk of syllabus to several parallel classes. I made a personal rule always to teach each class by a different method so that I didn't become stale – discussion-based learning for one group, problem-solving for another, didactic methods for a third and so on. The same principles apply for material repeated from year to year; good teachers cull the best of last year's work and then add improvements to it so that they are always honing their skills.

Falling rolls, of course, due to the fact that families are smaller nowadays, are causing contractions to the profession. This has changed the nature of teaching: promotion is slower, teachers stay longer in one post than they used to, schools are given less finance to equip themselves since this depends on a per-capita allowance which also takes account of the age of pupils. Currently there is an air of depression in the profession; in hard times many schools look uncared for and down at heel. Nevertheless, while striving for proper professional recognition and resources for education, teachers still reap many intrinsic rewards. Pupils can still be rewarding: their development intellectually and as maturing human beings is just as important in classrooms with peeling paint as in a showpiece building, perhaps more so.

Some intending teachers worry about the dependence of education on politics. Education policies are largely determined at Government level; finance for education comes from rates and is thus subject to the vagaries of local party politics. Many decisions about education seem to be decided not on educational criteria but upon those of party allegiance, financial constraint and political expedience. At the management level in education it becomes necessary to be fine-tuned to these issues, anticipating them and responding to them. Despite this comment on the political dependence of education it remains true that direct State interference and control of crucial aspects of teaching such as curriculum is less obtrusive in Britain than in most other developed countries.

Finally, young teachers are often concerned about whether to join a union, and if so, which one. My own view is that this is a matter of personal choice and the choice is not irrevocable. Before joining any union, find out about each one and exactly what it stands for. This should be done during your days as a trainee teacher, for union membership provides important insurance benefits once in employment – benefits and a form of protection you cannot do without. Which union you join, especially in the present climate, will probably depend on your own concept of professionalism. As well as a union you should seek out any professional association which will keep in touch with developments in your field, and invest a small sum in a subscription to this also. Most subject areas are supported by at least one such organization.

This overview has, perhaps, encouraged you to consider just a few of the questions that may have arisen in your mind as you have worked through this book and faced seriously the issue of whether you think teaching represents an attractive career prospect. The next chapter looks at how to apply to become a trainee teacher and more specifically at some longer-term issues about teaching as a career.

12

Routes and Structures

This chapter falls into two parts. Part 1 is called Routes, because it describes the steps on the road to entering the profession. Part 2 is called structures because it casts a rapid glance ahead to discover where the qualified teacher might look for a career pattern.

The layout of part 1 is in the form of question and answer. By breaking the material down in this way it is hoped that it will both be easy to follow and provide a rapid means by which the reader can refer back to specific issues within it.

In the second part of the chapter a more conventional narrative account is supplemented by a diagram (table 12.1) illustrating some possible career directions for teachers.

Wherever appropriate, cross-references are made throughout the chapter to other sections of the book where particular points are discussed or illustrated at greater length.

PART 1: ROUTES

1. How do I set about applying to a college of education?

First, you need to think through the issue as to whether a college of education/BEd route is the right one for you. The alternatives are discussed throughout part 1 of this chapter as well as in chapter 10. Then you must look at which colleges and courses are likely to be relevant to your needs. The answers to questions 2 and 3, below, will start you thinking.

A book designed to aid you in your decision-making

progress is: *The Handbook of Degree and Advanced Courses* published by NATFHE and available in libraries and careers offices.

If you decide to apply to a college of education you must do so through a so-called clearing house – i.e. a central office which supplies application forms and deals with completed applications. The clearing-house forms may be available to sixth-form students from their schools, but can be obtained from:

> The Clearing House Registry
> 3 Crawford Place
> London W1H 2BN

When you get the forms, work over them slowly, answer carefully, ghost your responses on to the forms in pencil, ink in the result when you are happy with what you have written.

2. *Are all colleges likely to be suitable to my needs and interests?*

In a word: no. There are a number of factors you will need to take into account. The first two are your choice of age range and the specialist subject(s) you wish to pursue.

Not every college runs courses for infant, junior and secondary age ranges. Some are primary only. Others may offer a number of quite flexible packages, usually engineered through course options and choices of teaching-practice location. For example, you may be able to select teaching practices with children of 10–11 and 12–13, so giving you a 'middle-school' experience. Or there may be a specific opportunity to spend all your time with the infant age group. Some colleges have built up a reputation for strength in a particular age-range, so ask teachers you know about any college you might be considering. Equally, it may be that a college with a generally good reputation has a particularly small or weak option course in one area. Size is not a wholly reliable guide: but students have been known to vote with their feet.

The age-range training a college offers may well affect its

curriculum, and hence the specialist subjects on offer to you. For example, a college which offers 'primary-only' courses may have evolved a BEd degree aimed at generalist teachers. Its graduates will emerge with a good grasp of pedagogical principles and with some knowledge of the whole primary curriculum; but they will not have any specialist skill. Other colleges offer more subject-oriented specialist courses. Which you choose is partly a matter for your own preference; but remember, in the profession your promotion is likely to depend in part at least on your having some specific and identifiable skill or strength. Initial generalist training only may be an excellent basis for teaching, but may be less attractive as a career prospect. If you acquire a specialist training early on, you can always abandon it later in favour of administration, counselling, or even a second specialism! Most potential secondary teachers see a subject specialism (perhaps with a subsidiary subject, too) as essential.

Teachers of some practical subjects – physical education is a prime example – also regard it as sensible to choose a course that offers also a classroom discipline. Many PE staff do not find the idea of outdoor work as appealing at 50 as they did at 30, so a second string is quite useful.

In addition, some colleges (and university departments) have built up a national reputation for one specific area of expertise. These areas can be diverse: craft courses, domestic science, physical education, religious education, history. Of course, if you want to specialize in one of these areas, you should apply in the first instance to an institution with a specialist reputation. If you cannot obtain a place, then you can move on to look at more general institutions that still provide a measure of specialist opportunity.

It should be emphasized, however, that what is being advocated here is not a narrow subject-based training. Rather, the watchword is: make sure your course is going to train you to do *something* well rather than everything in a colourless way. Bear in mind, too, that the current political climate is demanding of teachers more employment-oriented skills and more technological skills.

Do look at the prospectus of your chosen college to see

how firmly its feet are planted on the ground of the twentieth century. Any course that does not include some computer training is likely to be behind the times. Look, too, for mentions of things like audiovisual approaches to student and child education; specialist accommodation such as laboratories or simulated classrooms; the incidence of children visiting the college (as opposed to students visiting schools); and the part played by local teachers, heads and advisers in contributing to the courses. If all such mentions are lacking, give that college a miss.

You might also have a look at the list of academic staff which is usually included in the prospectus. Though one can't tell a lot from this, there are two judgments you can make.

First, look at the qualifications. Make sure that, as well as first degrees (BA, BSc) the vast majority of staff also possess PGCE or BEd teaching qualifications. A reasonable percentage should also have undertaken advanced study to obtain masters degrees in education [MEd, MA(Ed)] or in academic subjects, (MA, MSc). These degrees are often the result of advanced taught courses. In most universities the MPhil and PhD degrees are awarded for research in education and other academic disciplines. Since the BEd degree now contains a good deal of research in its Honours element, note how many staff have had direct research experience themselves.

The other judgment you can make about staff is to try to discover how many of them you can track down as active in contributing to the literature of education. Visit a large educational bookseller such as Foyles in London, or the Blackwell's University Bookshop on your local university campus. If you are looking for a place at an institution which specializes in science, go over the science education books. Do any of the staff in your chosen institution appear as authors? If not, where are the authors located? Would you be better off to apply there in the first instance?

In your assessment of a potential college don't forget to look at the senior staff: the principal and vice-principal. Are they well known? Do their views or doings appear in the *Times Educational Supplement* (see question 12) ever?

A final word: don't select a college by location – because it's near home or in pretty countryside. Rather, find out where its teaching practice schools are. If they are likely to give you at least some experience of the urban environment, relatively impoverished areas, multi-racial communities and the full range of pupils' abilities then they are likely to do you more professional good than those using two-teacher schools in stereotyped dormitory villages. For most teachers the realism of employment is with the former rather than the latter.

3. How can I found out about individual colleges?

In order to set about your application (see question 1), and to enable you to make an initial selection of colleges (see question 2), you need two things: a list of colleges and the time to send off for prospectuses from as many as possible that might interest you.

A list of colleges can be found in *The Handbook of Degree and Advanced Courses* (see question 1) or in *The Education Authorities Directory* published and updated annually by the School Government Publishing Company Ltd. This volume will be in your local reference library. If it isn't, your school may have a copy: it's the kind of book that would be kept in the secretary's office. In any event the librarian in your reference library will definitely be able to track down the information for you.

The *Directory* will give you the locations of all colleges of education, colleges of higher education and polytechnics with teacher-training departments. It will provide basic data about size, subject and age-range specialisms. From this basic data you will be able to compile an initial list of colleges which interest you (see also question 4).

Take the name and address of each possible college or department and write (to the Registrar) for a prospectus. When you have a collection of these, go through them bearing in mind the advice given throughout this chapter. Remember – a glossy brochure may indicate a professional approach by the institution, but still read between the lines.

4. What other factors should influence my choice?

In answer to question 2 it was suggested that you should take into account four factors initially: the suitability of the course to your personal needs, the quality and reputation of the college, the relevance of its courses to the contemporary education scene, and the quality of its staff. These factors will help you to establish a shortlist of colleges from those available. The issue of geographical location was touched upon also; especially as this affects the potential range and quality of practical learning experiences. Two more personal factors should also be taken into account.

The first relates to your leaving home – a circumstance that will apply to most young readers of this book. It is probably unwise to choose a college from which you can get home daily or even regularly at weekends. The temptation to do so may be strong and you will fail to give your course 7-days-a-week commitment. Equally, some young people find their parents put pressure on them to choose a college close by because the family has come to rely, for one reason or another, upon the daily presence of the son or daughter. My own experience with students has been that the greater the emotional pressure to remain near home the more imperative it is for the full adult maturity of the student that he or she learns to stand alone. While most students will have no problems on this score, some will find the issue acute and must persevere to see it through.

Second, the institution you choose ought to offer some hope of social activity; so look at the range of clubs, activities and similar opportunities on offer. Have an eye, too, to what is likely to be available in the local community. If you spend your free time climbing almost unassailable peaks then you might want to choose a college in undulating rural isolation. On the other hand, non-climbers could find the same location quite rivetingly boring by the end of 4 years.

Whichever college you choose you will spend the 4 most formative years of your young adulthood there so it is really important to make a good choice. Transfer between colleges

once your course has started can be arranged in some cases:
but many 'losing' institutions are reluctant so don't put any
hope on this as a back-stop to sensible selection initially.
Some primary colleges, for example, tend to be almost
single sex. Ask yourself if that's what you really want! Most
colleges of any merit try to put across a particular 'ethos': a
Christian community, student participation in decision-
making, superb craftsmenship, sporting prowess, or strong
discipline. Find an ethos that suits you – at least on paper.
When you go for interview (see questions 10 and 12) you
can check it out.

5. *Should I consider a BEd programme in a polytechnic?*

Yes. Until a few years ago teacher education was confined to
university departments and colleges of education. During
the 1970s many colleges of education were decreased in size
and amalgamated with other forms of higher education.
Thus training of the BEd kind can be found in many
polytechnics as well as colleges. These polytechnic departments usually maintain the facilities and traditions of the
former college or consortium of colleges.

Polytechnics, being large institutions with many departments, employ a wide spectrum of specialist staff. There
may well be advantages in this over, say, a now very small
(200- to 300-student) specialist college of education where
the whole of the work in a particular discipline may devolve
to one tutor. On the other hand polytechnics, by virtue of
size, may be more impersonal; though many are so sub-
divided as to compensate for this problem. The real answer
to this question is that one should explore what life is like
for a trainee teacher in any polytechnic which seems to be
suitable to one's needs. In terms of resources, Government
policies have recently favoured polytechnics, and so a course
here may be a worthwhile option.

All the points made about choosing a course in answer to
questions 2–4 apply equally here. Application to a polytechnic education course is via the route set out in answer to
question 1.

6. If I choose a degree-plus-PGCE route into teaching, how do I go about selecting a university for my degree course?

First of all, you need to decide what precisely you want to study. On this issue, here are a few thoughts.

Some degree subjects are regarded as wholly unsuitable for teachers; for example architecture or veterinary medicine. These simply don't feature on the school curriculum.

Some degree areas could be construed as suitable even though they don't appear in that form in school curricula: e.g. American Studies or Media Studies. Small numbers of graduates in these disciplines do enter teaching and provide a source of innovation. Job opportunities may well be limited.

Too many graduates are available in some disciplines, making competition for PGCE places and jobs very tough. This observation applies generally in the humanities (though less to English and RE perhaps than to history and geography); and also to social sciences.

Physics and mathematics are shortage subjects, so some preference may be given to applicants in these disciplines at the PGCE level. The Government is currently promoting all aspects of technology.

Other factors may colour the picture. There are still few women scientists; so an able woman physicist could find herself in high demand from schools.

Once you have made your choice of degree subject, what universities are available? Many universities cover a range of disciplines; but, like other institutions, universities have their specific strengths and weaknesses. A few are highly specialist in nature. Your careers teacher should be able to advise here; and recent graduates will often know what is good and what is less good in their own universities of origin.

Once again, universities issue their own prospectuses. By reading these, reading between the lines, looking at the size of the faculties, and exploring the bookshops as suggested in response to question 2, you will get some idea of the quality of the particular institution in your area of interest.

To take an obvious example, University B is likely to be more fruitful than University A for Spanish.

University A

Subject: Spanish

Staff: John Smith BA MLitt Senior Lecturer

Joan Brown BA Lecturer

Degrees offered: BA (Hons) full-time

Information: A new department within the Faculty of Modern Languages. Library and audio laboratory facilities are likely to be expanded over the next 3 years.

University B

Subject: Spanish

Staff: A. Bloggs BA MLitt PhD, professor and head of faculty

C. Devon MA PhD Senior Lecturer

E. Frogg BA MA MLitt Senior Lecturer

G. Hanks BA Lecturer

I. Jinks MA Lecturer

Laboratory technician: K. Lambert

Degrees offered: BA (Hons) full-time

MA part-time taught course

MLitt part-time research

PhD part-time research

Information: Spanish is offered as a degree course in its own right or as part of a combined modern-language degree with French or German. Students use the extensive and well-equipped language laboratories. The subject has been established for 10 years. All full-time students for the BA (Hons) degree in Spanish are expected to spend 6 months in Spain in approved educational activity during the second year of the course.

Once you have decided what university course is for you, you can find out which universities are potentially suitable by consulting one of the following books: Peter Wilby, *The Sunday Times Good University Guide* (Granada, St Albans, 1984) or K. Boehn and N. Wellings (eds), *The Student Book 85/86* (Macmillan, London, 1985). These volumes should be available in your Careers Library at school or at the reference library in your area, and are updated regularly.

Procedures for applying to universities are described in the answer to question 8.

General considerations for choosing a university are similar to those in the answers to questions 2 and 4.

You should notice that polytechnics as well as universities run degree courses. Perhaps you will find the right course for you in a polytechnic. From here, on graduating, you might read for your PGCE at a polytechnic or transfer to a university department of education. Thus polytechnics provide both the BEd and the degree-plus-PGCE routes into the profession. The advantages of the degree-plus-PGCE are considered in question 7.

7.   *What advantages has the degree-plus-PGCE route over a BEd degree?*

It is probably a matter of horses for courses. The traditional answer has been that the college/BEd route is more advantageous for primary teachers (since the concentration is on pedagogy), the BA/PGCE route in a polytechnic or university is more beneficial to secondary trainees (since the emphasis is on subject expertise). The distinction is too clear-cut to be valid, though it remains *broadly* true. You should also take several other factors into account.

First, matching your own preference and temperament to the right course for you is more important than a generalization such as those above.

Second, in some specialisms college courses are definitely to be preferred: this is generally true of infant education, and may be true in some subject areas such as art.

Third, Government policy at present seems to favour the degree-plus-PGCE route; but Governments change!

Fourth, in areas which have a middle-school (8–12 or 9–13/14) form of school organization the former primary generalist is often replaced by the specialist or semi-specialist.

Fifth, it will be recalled from chapter 8 that the degree route actually puts off the moment of decision about career-specific training. You may or may not consider that to be an advantage: certainly you won't encounter a pupil for 3 years if you decide to go to university.

You might also dwell on the fact that there have been a number of moves in recent years to provide first degrees of an integrated or non-specialist nature. These appear under such titles as General Arts or Combined Studies; and at first sight they look ideal for would-be primary teachers. Though a few such courses have attained a high national reputation, many have not. The major advantage of such degree 'packages' in Combined Studies is that they allow you to tailor your course to your own interests.

Make up your mind exactly which degree course you wish to follow *before* you approach a university or polytechnic, lest you end up like a young acquaintance of mine: he went to interview with an open mind and a good clutch of 'A' levels, but came away from his course with a degree in Hebrew and no idea what to do with it!

8. How do I apply for a university or polytechnic place to read for a BA or BSc degree?

Application to BEd courses of teacher training are dealt with through the clearing house referred to in answer to question 1. For BA/BSc and other first degrees available in polytechnics you should obtain the *Guide for Applicants* issued annually by:

Polytechnics Central Admissions System
PO Box 67
Cheltenham
Gloucestershire GL50 3AP

With your *Guide* will come an application form. The form is quite long and you should complete it carefully, first in pencil so that you can correct errors, and then ink it over.

The *Guide* is so detailed that it will answer all your questions about opportunities in polytechnics, which are exciting and worthy of careful study.

Similarly, entry to universities is now handled centrally. The address to write to is:

Universities Central Council on Admissions
PO Box 28
Cheltenham
Gloucestershire GL50 1HY

9. What qualifications will I require before I can apply to a college, polytechnic or university?

For a BEd degree course minimum qualifications at present are five separate GCE subjects, of which two must be at 'A' level. English and Maths are required at least to 'O' level. Of course, CSE grade-1 passes are accepted as 'O'-level equivalents. Some changes are likely in the requirements to accommodate the proposed GCSE which is to replace GCE and CSE exams – possibly in 1988 but perhaps a year or so later. Your careers teacher or careers officer will be able to keep you in touch with any changes.

For other degree subjects the situation is less clear cut. You will require five GCE subjects still, and at least two but usually three at 'A' level. If you have three 'A' levels with just one additional 'O' level you may be eligible. For a particular course you may be required to have passed a specific 'A' level, e.g. possession of English, Geography and History 'A' levels may not be acceptable for a degree in Chemistry or Languages. Where competition is fierce you may be required not only to pass 'A'-level exams but to do so at specified grades; and acceptance of you may be on condition of your obtaining those grades.

Mature students with non-standard qualifications can obtain entry to most courses; polytechnics and colleges of education may welcome such students. Fuller information is given in appropriate college prospectuses and clearing-house literature. The polytechnic literature is particularly helpful here.

10. If I secure an interview, how should I prepare for it?

First of all, confirm in writing that you will attend. Second, if you are attending for a BEd interview, you will have done a great deal already by having read this book!

Should your interview be for a BA/BSc place try to have read one or two textbooks at undergraduate level in your subject area. Also, make yourself *au fait* with any contemporary or popular debates in your discipline.

Go clean, smart, fairly formal, and be on time.

If possible, visit the institution beforehand to find your way around; but if this is impractical at least arrive early, explore the site, and try to get the 'feel' of the place.

Of course, you will feel nervous. But try hard to relax: the interviewer will *want* to take you rather than reject you, so don't blow your chances by being tongue-tied. Equally, don't talk for the sake of it. Think first.

How to conduct yourself during the interview is dealt with in answer to question 12.

11. . What form is such an interview likely to take?

As far as BEd courses go, the answer is rather varied. Typically, you might be asked to attend for a whole day. Such a day may include: a tour of the site, informal chat with existing students, a meal, a written test, an interview with one or more staff. This would be a good pattern since you would learn a lot about the institution and they would have time to assess you. It has to be said that interview methods are very variable, but you can often judge the quality of an institution by the care it gives to its interviewees.

12. Are there any helpful hints on handling interviews effectively?

Yes, there are a number of things you can do to help yourself during an interview. The pre-requisites are listed in the answer to question 10. In addition, you should consider the following.

The interviewer is likely to be making an assessment of your character, so think about the image you are conveying in the way you talk, the way you dress, and the way you gesticulate or sit. At worst, you could go mildly scruffy, slouch smoking or chewing gum in the deepest armchair, and talk non-stop about how you could do better a job than the average headteacher. But the interviewer will rather be looking to see

- if you have a warm, caring personality,
- if you have self-discipline and strength of purpose,
- if you have shown evidence of initiative and energy,
- if you can act, under pressure, in a natural and relaxed way,
- if you can show a touch of humour (but don't resort to the Irish joke you heard yesterday at the disco!).

He or she will also be looking for intellectual qualities.

- understanding and awareness of current issues,
- mature reflection and ability to see various viewpoints,
- academic interest and achievement.

In the light of this knowledge you ought to think out some of the more obvious interview questions, which might include:

- why do you wish to study this subject?
- why do you want to be a teacher?
- what appeals to you about this age group?
- why did you choose this college?
- what will you do if we don't offer you a place here?

A favourite last-resort question of interviewers is about one's hobbies or how the candidate spends his or her free time. While there may be something to be said for not telling the *whole* truth, it's also critical not to tell any lies! It's quite amazing how many alleged readers can't remember the title of the book they are currently perusing avidly, or how many film buffs don't know who directed the latest masterpiece and Hollywood award winner. If you really are into Heavy Metal, say so; and be prepared to explain who Bon Jovi are and the particular merits of their offerings as opposed to Def Leppard's.

You won't be able to prepare for the more inventive questions interviewers dream up. Don't be afraid to pause for a few seconds to compose a response rather than blurt out an answer or resort to 'ah', 'well', 'maybe'.

You should also go prepared with some questions of your own to ask interviewers. Most interviews end with an invitation for you to put your questions. To ask none is perhaps to lack initiative; to ask twenty could be excessive. Pre-select two. If nothing more pressing crops up, ask them. Some possible questions, which signal that you have thought things out, might be:

- what percentage of final-year students from this college secured jobs last year?
- what range of school experience will my course offer me if I'm accepted? (see question 2)
- how does the college help final-year students who are seeking employment?

If you are planning an interview for a BEd place a good piece of advice is to read the *Times Educational Supplement*, which is published weekly on Fridays and which gives all the latest professional news. You will need to do this for several months before your interview, so start now rather than leaving it until you have applied. The TES is quite expensive, but most public libraries stock it. A charitable teacher might agree to pass it on to you weekly if you express interest!

For some weeks before an interview you may find it helpful to jot down possible questions and your proposed answers – but don't take the notes with you on the day.

Finally, when the interview is over, spare a thought for the interviewer: he or she has probably seen a great many students. It doesn't come amiss to say 'thank-you' and 'goodbye' – even if you hope it will be *au revoir*!

13.   What about the financial side?

This is too big an issue to be dealt with here. In general, students proceeding from school are elegible for grant awards from the LEAs. Sadly, the level of grant depends on parental income – even though at 18 you have reached the age of majority!

General advice is: go in person to your LEA offices (address in phone book) and ask for details. Some produce a helpful booklet. If you still have queries, ask for an appointment and go to discuss the matter.

Mature students who have not received a grant previously may also be eligible for support: again, contact your LEA.

If you encounter problems you could seek advice from:

> The National Union of Students
> 461 Holloway Road
> London N7 6LJ

For sixth formers, general advice should be available from your careers teacher, who will be familiar with the local situation.

As soon as you are offered a college place, read the adverts put out by the major banks. Aware that a customer caught may be kept for life, they are only too willing to receive your grant cheque! Take the best deals on offer at the time; and remember that free services or concessions are worth more than plastic files or pretty cheque books.

14. Once I have secured a place, is there anything I ought to do by way of preparation for my course?

Yes. If the institution provides a preliminary book list, borrow the books from a library and read them. Make notes as you proceed. If it does not, write and ask if one is supplied or available. In the event of a negative response, consult the Further Reading section of this book if you have applied for a BEd course.

Sort out your financial affairs (see question 13). Get together any personal belongings you may need or wish to take to college with you.

Now you can enjoy your last vacation before you start on the career trail.

PART 2: STRUCTURES

In this section we are going to proceed on the assumption that you have successfully completed a period of training as described in chapter 10 and that you have entered the profession as a probationary teacher. After 1 year you should receive full qualified status. From now on the path of your career can be varied, and this section is designed to give you just a glimpse of the possibilities. The basic structure of the profession is shown in table 12.1.

As you look at table 12.1 a few words of explanation are in order. For convenience I have indicated the main route into and through the profession in column B; and you would enter it on the lowest rung. Column B represents the promotion ladder as it exists in the pay structure at the time of this book going to press, but there are moves afoot to change it. In particular many people would like to telescope Scales I and II into one long scale with automatic procedure along it by means of annual increments of pay: this would give a better career structure to young teachers. At present, each of the scales represents both a level of seniority, and also a level of pay from a minimum to a maximum through annual increments. Current levels of pay and increments are shown in table 12.2. Progress from one scale to another is by promotion only.

Scale 2, 3, 4 and Senior Teacher posts are given for increased responsibility in schools: this is considered in more detail later. All holders of these posts are teachers and undertake a major amount of face-to-face teaching in the classroom. Above this, roles become more managerial. What is not shown in the table for column B is that schools are allowed a specific number of scale posts according to numbers of pupils on roll and their ages. So small primary schools have very few scale posts and may have none above scale 2 or 3; large comprehensive schools will have more posts and posts at higher levels. In the same way, allocation of deputy-head posts is roll-dependent; remuneration for heads and deputies depends on size and type of school.

Table 12.1 *The structure of the profession*

LEA Advisory/ Inspection Service (A)	Main school route (B)	College of Education route (C)
Chief Adviser		
		Principal
Principal Adviser		
		Vice Principal
	Headteacher	
Senior Adviser	First Deputy	Head of Department
	Third or second deputy	Principal Lecturer
	Senior teacher	
Adviser	Scale IV with responsibilities for faculties, departments, year groups, etc.	Senior Lecturer
Advisory Teacher	Scale 3	Lecturer
	Scale 2	
	Scale 1/ Probationer	

Polytechnic Education Department (D)	University Education Department (E)	Government Inspectorate (HMI) (F)
		Chief Inspector
	Professor	
Director		Staff Inspector
	Reader	
Deputy Director		District Inspector
Head of Department/ Reader	Senior Lecturer	
		Inspector
Principal Lecturer		
Senior Lecturer	Lecturer	
Lecturer II		
Lecturer I		

Table 12.2 *Salary scales (at the time of going to press)*

Teachers

This table shows the salary which will come into effect from 31 March 1986 if the agreement is ratified in the Burnham Primary and Secondary and CLEA/st Committees.

Scale 1	Scale 2	Scale 3	Scale 4	ST*	Salary £
0					5904
1					6177
2					6384
3					6588
4	0				6783
5	1				7041
6	2				7305
7	3				7569
8	4				7845
9	5				8118
10	6	0			8391
11	7	1			8685
12	8	2			8985
13	9	3			9282
	10	4	9642		
	11	5	0		9984
	12	6	1		10413
		7	2	0	10758
		8	3	1	11160
		9	4	2	11565
		10	5	3	11970
			6	4	12372
			7	5	12945
			8	6	13413
				7	14064
				8	14535

*ST = Senior Teacher

		Deputy heads			
Group†	Point	Salary £	Group†	Point	Salary £
Below	0	7386		3	12819
4	1	7680		4	13152
	2	7971	8	0	12372
	3	8256		1	12717
	4	8547		2	13062
	5	8838		3	13410
	6	9126		4	13758
	7	9414			
	8	9705	9	0	13062
	9	9999		1	13410
	10	10290		2	13758
	11	10581		3	14106
4	0	8733		4	14490
	11	9030	10	0	13932
	2	9318		1	14286
	3	9615		2	14643
	4	9912		3	14997
	5	10200		4	15315
	6	10491	11	0	14643
	7	10788		1	14997
	8	11082		2	15345
	9	11373		3	15693
5	0	9771		4	16047
	1	10113	12	0	15474
	2	10464		1	15822
	3	10803		2	16185
	4	11145		3	16539
	5	11490		4	16890
	6	11829	13	0	15945
	7	12177		1	16305
6	0	11145		2	16659
	1	11490		3	17013
	2	11829		4	17373
	3	12177			
	4	12492	14	0	16674
7	0	11778		1	17031
	1	12123		2	17386
	2	12474		3	17751
				4	18108

		Heads			
Group	Point	Salary £	Group[†]	Point	Salary £
1	0	10388		4	16251
	1	10683	8	0	15909
	2	10977		1	16260
	3	11271		2	16620
	4	11559		3	16968
2	0	10839		4	17319
	1	11127	9	0	17133
	2	11421		1	17496
	3	11718		2	17847
	4	12015		3	18204
3	0	11343		4	18567
	1	11634	10	0	18255
	2	11931		1	18606
	3	12222		2	18969
	4	12516		3	19323
4	0	12057		4	19683
	1	12402	11	0	19704
	2	12747		1	20061
	3	13089		2	20433
	4	13437		3	20796
5	0	13065		4	21168
	1	13413	12	0	21090
	2	13761		1	21552
	3	14106		2	22008
	4	14448		3	22467
6	0	13983	13	0	22221
	1	14343		1	22686
	2	14682		2	23145
	3	15039		3	23604
	4	15390			
7	0	14850	14	0	23502
	1	15207		1	23967
	2	15552		2	24426
	3	15900		3	24891

[†] Group numbers refer to the size of school.

Lecturers
(Salaries applicable from 1 April 1985)

Point	Salary £	Point	Salary £
Lecturer I/IA			
0	6207	7	11220
1	6462	8	11733
2	6726	9	12216
3	6990	10	12705
4	7251		
5	7536	**Senior Lecturer**	
6	7806	0	11733
7	8121	1	12216
8	8439	2	12705
9	8751	3	13239
10	9066	4	13785
11	9372	5	14280
12	9675	6	14763
13	9972		
14	10266	**Principal**	
15	11037‡	**Lecturer/**	
		Reader	
Lecturer II		0	13479
0	7926	1	14247
1	8412	2	14745
2	8886	3	15309
3	9357	4	15801
4	9816	5	16302
5	10260	6	16800
6	10764	7	17289

‡ LIs on the maximum of the scale to progress to point 7 of the LII scale as though the scales were continuous w.e.f. 1 September 1985. Similar arrangements for Lecturer IA to be notified.

There is, therefore, a good deal of flexibility or overlap within the system.

Columns C–E indicate how a teacher with experience may move into a training role in a college, polytechnic or university department. Although the columns are set against the school structure in column B the levels of seniority and payment are not meant to be taken as anything like exact equivalents. The same comment applies to columns A and F. Thus, if we compare columns B and A, though it is unlikely to be the case that an advisory teacher will be appointed until he or she has had good classroom experience, a scale-2 teacher might be so appointed, and an advisory teacher might well be paid above scale 3. The point is that there are possibilities for transfer between the branches of the education service, not that transfer works on an inflexible principle of 'rank for rank'. So let us examine the various branches in more detail.

Column B might be labelled the traditional school route through the profession. You enter as a probationer, and climb the ladder a step at a time. In the middle grades of your career – scales 2–4 – there are many possible specialisms you can follow. Here are some typical examples:

Scale 2
- in a primary school, responsible for a subject area as a consultant to other staff.
- in a secondary school, as head of a small year group.
- in a secondary school, responsible for a specific administrative task.

Scale 3
- in a primary school, perhaps the most senior staff member.
- in a large comprehensive school, the head of a small subject department or the deputy in a large one.
- in a comprehensive school, a specialist teacher responsible school-wide for audiovisual education or for remedial pupils.
- in a comprehensive school, the head of a very large year group.

| Scale 4 | ● in a comprehensive school, the head of lower school years (years 1 and 2) or the head of a Faculty or large department or responsible for the careers education of all pupils. |
| Senior Teacher | ● In a comprehensive school, the most senior member of staff, possibly in charge of the sixth form and the examination administration; a member of the senior management team. |

Experience in the higher grades of teacher scale will qualify you to apply for a deputy headship and eventually a headship. These roles give teachers an opportunity to undertake mainly administrative duties. There is currently much debate as to whether it is logical to reward able classroom teachers by promoting them to roles in which teaching as such barely features. The fact is, many people in all walks of life do enjoy the management aspects of their jobs and like to graduate to this. It would be sensible if the top rewards could be open to two kinds of professional: those with mainly teaching roles and those with mainly administrative ones.

We have now made the journey up ladder B, but many teachers migrate sideways during their careers. Some become trainers, and thus join ladders C, D or E – and, of course, once in this role they can transfer between these three. In all training roles teachers need to be both good practitioners and good academics. The job specification of a trainer has been described in chapter 9. Once again, those who reach the highest levels in these training roles shoulder major administrative burdens. It is also true that a considerable variety of tasks is open to trainers. Some typical roles are listed to give you the flavour of the job.

| Lecturer | ● may specialize in an academic subject; or in a branch of education such as sociology; or may teach both kinds of course; or may have a particular specialism such as special education, |

multicultural education or educational administration. He or she will be responsible for a group of students during teaching practice; the job will also require a level of pastoral care.

Senior Lecturer or Principal Lecturer	● In addition to teaching may have course responsibilities and will be active in curriculum development and administration. He or she may have held a special post such as tutor in charge of in-service courses.
Head of Department	● will be responsible on a day-to-day basis for all teaching, administration and welfare of staff and students in his or her area of work. Major role is initiating new courses and in providing leadership and maintaining teaching standards.
Professor	● as well as head of department role, the professor will have extensive administrative responsibility, will be expected to represent his or her institution nationally and will provide a high standard of scholarship. His or her job will involve national and probably international travel to professional engagements.

An alternative route from teaching into training is represented by column A. Each LEA maintains an advisory service to teachers; in some areas the rather old-fashioned label 'inspector' is used instead. The LEA advisers have a number of functions, but primarily they monitor local standards of education. Each advisory service is staffed and organized differently. Some appoint mainly subject advisers; others appoint to school age ranges. The advisory team, however constituted, has to include coverage of all age ranges from nursery to 18 and all subject areas likely to be encountered in the Authority. Advisers may be appointed from the ranks of heads, teachers or trainers, and advisory staff have their own internal promotion structures which vary somewhat from Authority to Authority.

Teachers' Centres, largely established in the 1960s and 1970s though often closed now in response to financial constraints, are local resource bases where in-service training sessions are held and where teachers can keep up-to-date on resource materials. They are provided by the LEA; and centre wardens may be paid as teachers, or heads or advisers according to their levels of responsibility. The role involves both training and organization, and obviously demands a postholder who is *au fait* with a broad sweep of age-range and curriculum provision.

The responsibility for education in this country rests ultimately with the Department of Education and Science whose officers are known as Her Majesty's Inspectors of Schools (HMIs). HMIs are recruited from all branches of the profession, and they inspect all kinds of education and training covered in this book as well as quite specialist activities such as education in prisons. HMIs have their own grade structure (not fully described here), are largely peripatetic and cover vast areas of the country every week. They are often away from home and base for long periods, and include among their many duties the inspection of and reporting on whole schools. Their reports of such inspections are now published, copies can be purchased from Her Majesty's Stationery Office (HMSO), and summaries appear regularly in the *Times Educational Supplement*.

From this brief, and by no means exhaustive survey, you will see that teaching can be made a very varied career and that it is not as stereotyped as many people imagine. To succeed you need all those qualities that apply in industry or commerce: skill, the ability to learn new techniques, energy, determination, hard work, enthusiasm. Teachers also need to care. It would be impossible to describe a typical career. Many who enter teaching at scale 1 end their professional days as a teacher on a higher scale; others aspire to and achieve headships; others move into the training or advisory roles. Oddly, it is hard to move back from say a lectureship in education into a practical teaching role in school – this is to be deplored, for such two-way traffic would be invaluable. I have not described all the avenues open within the education system: to do so would be too long and complicated. But perhaps if I describe my own career pattern to date you will understand something of the range of possibilities.

My teaching career began in 1963 as a secondary-school probationer in a London Borough. After three years I moved schools to become head of a small subject department in another secondary school, and began also to take a major share of responsibility for slow learners in the upper school. From there I moved to a college of education, as lecturer and later senior lecturer in a subject department training primary and secondary teachers; but after 5 years I had the opportunity to take charge of audiovisual education and services in the college. In 1976 I moved to Nottingham University to work for the Department of Education and Science in a project to research into and to develop training materials for secondary education. After 4 years my next post was as Principal Lecturer for educational research in a college specializing in primary education; but as my main interests lay with developing materials I returned to work in a university for the Schools Council (now the School Curriculum Development Committee), again writing materials for in-service education. In 1984 I joined a College of Further and Higher Education as Head of the Department of Applied Social Sciences, where the insights of subjects like sociology and psychology are brought to bear on professional training for groups as diverse as practising teachers and social workers, pre-nursing students and nursery nurses.

Not everyone would envy, or even want, such a varied career. Certainly it has involved many hours of study to qualify in new areas and much re-training to cope with widely divergent age groups. But obviously it does tend to illustrate that teaching, like life, accords with the Old Chinese proverb: what you get out of it depends on what you put into it. What *you* want out of it depends very much on your personality and attitudes.

Conclusion

Now that you have read this book you should have at your disposal knowledge which perhaps you did not have before. First, you will probably know by now whether or not you still find the thought of joining the teaching profession an attractive one. If you do, you will have a good idea of how to go about applying for a course of teacher training. Should you find yourself on a training course you will probably have discovered a good deal about its pattern and its content from the chapters which you have just read.

The purpose of this book has been to equip you with these three essential pieces of knowledge. In addition you should be more confident after reading the book to approach an interview at a training institution. What you have discovered will enable you to talk sensibly to the interviewer both about the career on which you intend to embark and also about the course of training that leads to it. You ought to be able to convince an interviewer both that you have made a firm decision and commitment to the profession, and also that you have a clear and realistic idea of what both the immediate and the longer-term future will hold if you become a member of it.

Perhaps the book will have served one other purpose: to have implanted in your mind a range of possibilities about the shape of your career in teaching should you achieve your goal. Certainly one message of the book has been that teaching can be varied, demanding and personally fulfilling.

Notes to the Chapters

1 Let's visit a Classroom

The material used in this reconstructed lesson account was observed in a classroom which I visited while I was Co-ordinator of the project 'Developing Pupils' Thinking Through Topic Work' financed by the Schools Council, now the School Curriculum Development Committee. During the project, lesson accounts were collected as case studies of effective topic work in action, and the insights gained were used to train other teachers. The account collected here uses observed material more freely, portraying accurately the flavour of the lesson without necessarily appearing in the format that would be used for research purposes. I have chosen this lesson because (although no lesson is ever perfect) it is an example of good teaching and effective learning. Involvement in a research project or/ with research for a higher degree is just one of the activities open to teachers to give their careers more variety. The point is taken up again in Chapter 12 (part 2).

2 A History of Education in Britain

In this chapter I have drawn heavily on an elderly but fascinating text: S. J. Curtis's *History of Education in Great Britain*, 7th edition (University Tutorial Press, London, 1967). A useful survey of the last seventy-five years can be found in a handy form in the *Times Educational Supplement* special commemorative insert '75 years of the TES', published in 1985 and available in libraries.

References

1 Bede, *Ecclesiastical History*, vol. 3, p. 18.
2 These lines are part of a longer poem called 'An Evening

Contemplation in College', published in a satirical magazine called *Oxford Sausage*, edited by Thomas Warton (1728–90), who later became Poet Laureate.

3 Insights from Psychology

References

1 J. W. Getzels in an article called *'Distinctive characteristics of able learners'* in *Maximal Reading Growth among Able Learners* (University of Chicago Press, Chicago, 1954), pp. 16–21.

2 G. D. Stoddard, *The Meaning of Intelligence* (Macmillan, London, 1945), p. 95.

3 Jean Piaget's work is difficult to read and understand. A place to begin might be with a text which explains some Piagetian work quite simply, such as N. Isaacs' book *The Growth of Understanding in the Young Child* (Ward Lock, London, 1961). Among Piaget's own books, one could try *Science of Education and the Psychology of the Child* (Longman, London, 1970).

4 Two books by Ronald Goldman are published by Routledge and Kegan Paul; they are *Religious Thinking from Childhood to Adolescence* (1964) and *Readiness for Religion* (1965).

5 W. A. Da Silva's work is contained in an article, 'The formation of historical concepts through contextual ones', *Birmingham Educational Review*, 24(3) (1972), pp. 197–211.

6 D. P. Ausubel was co-author with F. G. Robinson of *School Learning*, Holt, Rinehart and Winston, 1969. Ausubel has been an influential figure in education and psychology over several decades both in America and in Britain.

7 D. E. Broadbent's early work is contained in his book, *Perception and Communication*, Pergamon Press, Oxford, 1958. An updated review of his work on attention and perception can be found in 'Cognitive psychology and education', *British Journal of Educational Psychology*, 45 (1975), pp. 162–76.

8 B. F. Skinner is famous for his work on so-called 'behavioural' theories in psychology: he used birds and animals in experiments which led him to a view of learning that emphasized a learning process characterized by short steps, rapid reinforcement by reward, and correctly emitted responses to be established before learning could proceed. His work on language appeared in *Verbal Behaviour* (Appleton-Century-Crafts, New York, 1957).

9 Noam Chomsky is one of the foremost names in psychology and linguistics. His influence is discussed in *Chomsky* by J. Lyons in the Fontana Modern Masters series (1970), and in Part 1 of *Language* by R. C. Oldfield and J. C. Marshall in the Penguin Modern Psychology Readings series (1970).

10 Lev Semonovich Vygotsky, a Russian, was the author of a seminal volume, *Thought and Language* (MIT Press, Cambridge, Massachusetts, 1962).

11 Sigmund Freud (1856–1939) is known as the father of depth psychology. His theories are still enormously controversial. A useful book about Freud is Richard Wollheim's *Freud* (Fontana Modern Masters, 1971). This short and interesting summary refers to all Freud's works in detail and gives them context.

12 The name of C. G. Jung is often linked to Freud's. Among his best known works are *Man and His Symbols* (Picador, London, 1978) and *Memories, Dreams, Reflections* (Collins, London, 1983).

13 Hans Eysenck's theories of personality began with research he conducted among psychiatric patients at Maudsley Hospital, London. One important theoretical text by Eysenck is *The Structure of Human Personality* (Methuen, London, 1953). Eysenck developed a Personality Inventory which required respondents to choose reactions to specific statements of behaviour. According to the responses Eysenck established that subjects could be rated on the three dimensions of his EPI (already described in the main text). The EPI was widely used by researchers in the fields of psychology, sociology and education as it was quick to score and easy to administer. Results could be correlated with other kinds of data. More recently, Eysenck has become involved in controversies surrounding genetic inheritance of intelligence.

14 R. B. Cattell extended Eysenck's concept of a personality inventory and developed his own based on sixteen personality factors. The Cattell system for assessing personality is described in detail in R. B. Cattell, *The Technical Handbook to the 16PF* (Institute for Personality and Achievement Tests, Illinois, 1970). Like EPI, 16PF proved popular with researchers, who attempted to find connections between personality and other variables in the subjects they studied.

15 Carl Rogers's best known contribution to the styles of teaching and learning debate is *Freedom to Learn*.

Notes to the Chapters

4 Psychology at Work in Education

I am particularly grateful to acknowledge the permission given to me to quote extensively from a chapter contributed by Belle Wallace to my book *Finding and Helping the Able Child* (Croom Helm, Bexley, 1983). Belle Wallace's study of John is an excellent example of teachers, parents and specialist agents working in partnership for the good of the child, and as such it reflects the professionalism to which teachers must aspire.

5 The Social Bases of Education

Though it is a very long book, I would recommend that you read the whole of the *Social Life* study referenced in the text. It is a good example of large-scale research; it contains countless insights into the background of young children, and these insights are just as crucial to the teacher of adolescents as they are to the nursery teacher. This kind of study fixes education in the broad and detailed context of society, and helps to keep teachers aware of the complicated and far-reaching nature of the job.

References

1   Ginsberg's analysis appears in *The Study of Society*, ed. F. C. Bartlett (Kegan Paul, London, 1939). However, the book is dated and you can gain all you need of the theory from W. J. H. Sprott's book (see below).
2   W. J. H. Sprott's small book *Sociology* in the Hutchinson University Library Series (1966) has the advantage of clarity.
3   Basil Bernstein's theoretical work on language and social class appeared in a series of journal articles. A good review of Bernstein's developing theory remains that by Dennis Lawton: *Social Class, Language and Education* (Routledge and Kegan Paul, London, 1970).

6 Issues and Values in Education

I have tended to gloss over those writers and educators who have questioned aspects of traditional schooling. The temptation would be to follow them on a long detour, but this short text does not permit that luxury. However, you might like to read: L. Berg, *Death of a Comprehensive School* on Michael Duane's Risinghill (Penguin, London, 1968); J. Holt, *How Children Fail* (Penguin,

215

London, 1984); and A. S. Neill, *Summerhill* (Penguin, London, 1976).

References

1 William James, *Pragmatism* (Longman, London, 1907), p. 200.
2 The quotation is a summary of Dewey's view from S. J. Curtis and M. E. A. Boultwood, *A Short History of Educational Ideas*, 4th edition (UTP, London, 1965), p. 463.
3 A. W. Beck, *The Philosophy of Education* (Studyguide Series, Nottingham University School of Education, Nottingham, 1980).
4 Green Papers are discussion papers produced by Her Majesty's Stationery Office (HMSO) intended as a collection of the views of interested parties prior to seeking legislation (i.e. a White Paper stage). This particular Green Paper was published in 1985.
5 John Holt's work is typified in his books *How Children Fail* (Penguin, London, 1984) and *How Children Learn* (Penguin, London, 1984).
6 Ivan Illich's views can be found in his book *Deschooling Society* (Calder and Boyars, London, 1972).
7 The Certificate of Pre-Vocational Education (Consultative document, Joint Board for Pre-Vocational Education, London, May 1984).

7 Teaching Young Children

The Oracle Project, based at Leicester University, has produced several volumes of findings about primary schools. You might like to sample these by reading M. Galton, B. Simon and P. Croll, *Inside the Primary Classroom* and *Progress and Performance in the Primary Classroom*, both published in 1980 by Routledge and Kegan Paul, London.

8 Teaching Adolescents

Reference

1 The Rutter Report is in fact a volume of findings from a substantial study of secondary schooling; the M. Rutter et al., *Fifteen Thousand Hours: Secondary Schools and Their Effects on Children* (Open Books, London, 1979).

9 Teaching Beyond School

The issues that concern teachers at the further and higher education levels are sometimes rather different from those that occupy the minds of teachers in schools. You might care to find a copy of the *Times Higher Education Supplement* in your local library and read it to get the flavour; it is published every Friday.

10 Training for Teaching

Reference

1 Two rather dated, but still worthwhile, paperbacks which touch on issues relating to teachers in the early years are *The First Year of Teaching* and *Young Teachers and Reluctant Learners*, both by C. Hannam, P. Smyth and N. Stephenson, both published by Penguin, in 1976 and 1971 respectively.

11 Is Teaching for Me?

Some students have told me that they have been encouraged and helped by M. Marland's *The Craft of the Classroom* (Heinemann, London, 1975).

12 Routes and Structures

One issue which should be considered is that relating to conditions of service. This is, perhaps, especially important to women, who need to consider things like maternity leave or opportunity to return to work after having raised a family. Since this kind of information tends to date quickly I have not dealt with it in the text. My advice is to approach one of the teacher unions who have paid experts to advise on these issues. The major unions are:

National Union of Teachers (NUT)
Hamilton House
Mabledon Place
London   WC1H 9BD

National Association of Schoolmasters/
Union of Women Teachers (NAS/UWT)
Education Centre
Hillscourt
Rose Hill
Birmingham B45 8RS

Assistant Masters & Mistresses Association (AMMA)
29 Gordon Square
London   WC1H 0PX

Professional Association of Teachers (PAT)
99 Friar Gate
Derby   DE1 1EZ

Recommended Reading

The following suggestions are meant simply to start you off in preparing for your BEd or PGCE course. If your college or university department sends you a list of recommended reading (see page 198), use that instead. If not, these volumes may be helpful. Each contains further references.

On psychology of education

D. Child, *Psychology and the Teacher* (Holt, Rinehart and Winston, London, 1981)

On sociology of education

R. Meighan, *A Sociology of Education* (Holt, Rinehart and Winston, London, 1981)

On selected aspects of education

L. Cohen and L. Manion, *Perspectives on Classrooms and Schools* (Holt, Rinehart and Winston, London, 1981)

On philosophy of education

A. Beck, *An Introduction to the Philosophy of Education* (Studyguide series: Nottingham University School of Education, 1980)

On recent research

N. Bennett and C. Desforges, *Recent Advances in Classroom Research* (BJEP Monograph series no 2, Scottish Academic Press, Edinburgh, 1985)

E. C. Wragg, *Classroom Teaching Skills* (Croom Helm, Bexley, 1984)

Recommended Reading

On classroom skills

The seven volumes listed in the FOCUS series from Macmillan Education, Basingstoke are all valuable.

E. C. Wragg, *Class Management* (1981)

Trevor Kerry and M. K. Sands, *Mixed Ability Teaching* (1982)

Trevor Kerry, *Teaching Bright Pupils* (1981)

Peter Bell and Trevor Kerry, *Teaching Slow Learners* (1982)

Trevor Kerry, *Effective Questioning* (1982)

George Brown and Neville Hatton, *Explanations and Explaining* (1981)

Trevor Kerry and M. K. Sands, *Handling Classroom Groups* (1982)

You might also look at C. Sutton, *Communicating in the Classroom* (Hodder and Stoughton, London, 1981)

On subject studies

Select an appropriate title from the Focus on Education series from Macmillan Education:

John Partington and Pat Luker, *Teaching Modern Languages* (1984)

Trevor Kerry, *Teaching Religious Education* (1984)

John Nichol, *Teaching History* (1984)

Keith Selkirk, *Teaching Mathematics* (1984)

Christine Daniels and Ursula Hobson, *Teaching Home Economics* (1985)

M. K. Sands and Richard Hull, *Teaching Science* (1985)

Peter King, *Teaching English* (1985)

H. Tolley and F. Molyneux, *Teaching Geography* (forthcoming)

Jon Nixon, *Teaching Drama* (forthcoming)

On the infant school

D. Fontana, *The Education of the Young Child* (Blackwell, Oxford, 1984)

On the primary school

C. Richards, *New Directions in Primary Education* (The Falmer Press, Sussex, 1982)

On the comprehensive school

S. Ball, *Comprehensive Schooling: a reader* (The Falmer Press, Sussex, 1984).

On skills in higher education

G. Brown, *Lecturing and Explaining* (Methuen, London, 1976)

Index

221

curriculum, 14, 20, 70, 131, 177
Dahl, R., 62
Dalton plan, 100
Da Silva, W., 44
day care, 74, 80
degrees
  BA, 152, 164, 186, 192, 193
  BEd, 149, 152–4, 161–5, 180,
    183, 185, 186, 189, 192–5
  BSc, 152, 164, 186, 193
  in combined studies, 193
  in general arts, 193
  MA, 186
  MEd, 127, 149, 186
  MSc, 186
  PhD, 186
department, 132
Department of Education and
  Science, 116, 209
deputy head, 115, 120, 131,
  132, 166, 169, 200
Dewey, J., 26, 99, 100, 101, 110
discipline, 135, 140, 142, 169
discovery learning, 110, 129
disrupted family, 79
drives, 46
drug abuse, 176
Duane, M., 98

education
  elementary, 22
  further, 26, 144, 151
  higher, 144–51, 152–64
  history of, 16–30
  nursery, 58, 80, 113
  philosophy of, 16, 95–116
  primary, 4–15, 26, 42, 98,
    117–30
  psychology of, 16, 31–57,
    58–71
  secondary, 26, 131–43
  selective, 25, 26, 107
  sociology of, 16, 72–94

  vocational, 110, 111
Education Acts
  1870, 22
  1902, 23
  1944, 26, 27, 112
Education Welfare Officers, 48
educational priority areas, 28
educational psychologist, 62
elaborated code, 82, 83, 84
Emile, 97
emotional needs, 68
environment, 38, 52, 58, 59
extroversion, 56
Eysenck, H., 55, 114

faculty structure (FE/HE), 145
falling rolls, 105, 106, 181
family grouping (vertical
  grouping), 119
FE Teachers' Certificate, 145
first encounters, 89, 90
formal operations, 43, 44, 139
Freud, S., 54, 55

GCE, 27, 110, 133, 139, 148,
  194
GCSE, 110
gender, 87, 89, 113
genetics, 41
genotype, 37
Gestalt school, 60
Getzels, J., 38
Ginsberg, M., 72
Goldman, R., 43, 44
grammar schools, 19, 20, 22,
  23, 131
grants, 197
groups, 25, 136, 137
  in primary school, 4–15

Hadow Report, 24, 25
head of department, 140, 169
  in FE/HE, 145, 208, 210